The Andrew R. Cecil Lectures on Moral Values in a Free Society

established by

The University of Texas at Dallas

Volume IV

THE SEARCH FOR JUSTICE

The Search for Justice

WILLIAM H. WEBSTER
ANDREW R. CECIL
BARRY BAILEY
EWELL E. MURPHY, JR.
W. W. ROSTOW
KENNETH W. THOMPSON

With an Introduction by
ANDREW R. CECIL

Edited by
W. LAWSON TAITTE

The University of Texas at Dallas
1983

Library of Congress Catalog Card Number 83-080468
International Standard Book Number 0-292-77579-2

Distributed by the University of Texas Press,
Box 7819, Austin, Texas 78712

FOREWORD

Leaders and scholars of national recognition met in Dallas during the week of November 8, 1982, for the fourth annual Andrew R. Cecil Lectures on Moral Values in a Free Society. The purpose of this lecture series is to reexamine the fundamental values on which our nation is based and to ensure that these values are understood and preserved. This important educational program reaches beyond practical concerns and offers an opportunity to analyze the philosophical and moral basis of a free society.

It is our belief that an institution of higher learning has the responsibility to prove such a forum in which public values may be examined and debated. To this end, the lecture series was established in February 1979 and named for Dr. Andrew R. Cecil, the University's Distinguished Scholar in Residence and Chancellor Emeritus of The Southwestern Legal Foundation. As President of the Foundation, his leadership of that institution earned him the highest respect in educational and legal circles through the United States. Upon becoming Chancellor Emeritus of the Foundation, Dr. Cecil consented to serve as Distinguished Scholar in Residence at The University of Texas at Dallas. The Lectures are aptly named for an individual who, throughout his career, has addressed the central moral values of his time, always stressing a faith in the dignity and worth of every individual.

The 1982 Lectures focused on the topic "The Search for Justice." Dr. Cecil was joined by a theologian, a historian, a lawyer, an economist, a political scientist, and a judge and Director of the Federal Bureau of Investigation. Each of these men, prominent in his field of discipline, discussed in depth the virtue of justice, indispensable for the preservation of public order.

UTD is grateful to all who have made the Lectures a vital part of the tradition of our campus. I extend special thanks to Messrs. Bailey, Cecil, Murphy, Rostow, Thompson, and Webster for their willingness to share their knowledge and talents.

The University is also indebted to the supporters of the Cecil Lectures. Their contributions are enabling a continuation of a series of vital national importance. Through their generosity we are also delighted to be able to publish these proceedings of the 1982 Lectures.

I am confident that the readers will find that this fourth volume of the Cecil Lectures, *The Search for Justice*, will illuminate many important issues facing our society and the international community.

ROBERT H. RUTFORD, President
The University of Texas at Dallas

January 1983
Dallas, Texas

CONTENTS

INTRODUCTION

by

Andrew R. Cecil

Justice, observed Hamilton in the *Federalist,* is a highly ranked object of government. "Justice is the end of government. It is the end of civil society. It ever has been and ever will be pursued until it be obtained or until liberty be lost to pursuit." (*Federalist 51.*) The justice to which Hamilton refers, as the context suggests, is primarily concerned with the protection of economic interests and may have little in common with the traditional philosophical understanding of this term (to mention only Plato, for whom a just society is a perfect society). Nevertheless, the statement underscores the role of government in nurturing justice. The desire for justice is natural and is possessed universally by all mankind, but it is not a simple matter to define the laws of justice by which human affairs are to be regulated. There seems to be an agreement with the general precept offered by Aristotle that justice has some natural and universal core. There seems also to be a disagreement as to the source of the phenomenon known as a "sense of justice."

Some believe that justice connotes a form of intuition that supplies man with guidance for right conduct. Kant offers the presupposition of an *a priori* moral law. He called the supreme moral principle

11

which man ought to follow the "categorical imperative," which is the unconditional command of the
conscience: "Act as if the maxim from which you act
were to become through your will a universal law of
nature." The moral imperative, according to Kant, is
absolute and the moral sense innate, not derived
from questionable self-experiences; we act in obedience to this inner sense of justice, which commands
our behavior.

Others, known as empiricists, hold that there is no
moral faculty as such which distinguishes between
just and unjust, right and wrong, but that all our
knowledge comes from experience and through our
senses. Locke believed that sense-experience be-
gets ideas of right and wrong. Justice and morality
have no foundation in nature, and the sense of justice
is not innate but acquired.

According to Thomas Hobbes, who defended the
doctrine of absolute sovereignty, "justice and injustice are none of the faculties neither of the body nor
mind." He believed that they are qualities that relate
to man in society, and society is brought about by
man's need of security. Without an established civil
society, there would be perpetual warfare caused by
man's passion to acquire wealth "for so long as he can
keep it."

Two of the six purposes set forth in the Preamble of
our Constitution are to "establish justice" and to
"insure domestic tranquility." We must achieve both
of these goals if we are to succeed in having an
orderly society. Internal dangers demand the same
awareness and response as external threats. Violence

at home is dangerous since it divides the people into hostile camps and jeopardizes some of our most precious traditions and institutions. No society can remain free if its people live in fear of their fellowmen.

Attempts to control violence by coercive measures could turn us into a repressive society, and—as experience shows—repression nurtures within itself seeds of violent reaction. The fewer restrictions that surround individual liberties, the more successful is democracy. Restrictions are, however, justified for the preservation of the public health, safety, and morals. No less dangerous than repression is anarchy. Great civilizations have fallen less often from external assault than from the internal decay which anarchy brings about. One of the great challenges of our times is to insure "domestic tranquility" by preserving the important freedoms of our open society—freedom from harm and freedom from fear.

Judge William H. Webster, in his "Liberty and Justice for All: Keeping the Scales in Balance," emphasizes that it is possible to harmonize the values of order and freedom. If an imbalance between them arises, our legal system has legislative and judicial remedies to correct it. Our object should be that fairness—judged by contemporary standards—be done, and be seen to be done. This object is essential because in a democracy justice is predicated on public trust in the law and its enforcement.

Judge Webster points out areas in which law enforcement officials and the judicial system have had new burdens imposed on them in recent years but denies that these represent an insuperable imbalance at the expense of justice. Law enforcement

officials also have a great variety of new techniques
to aid them in their duties, and it is important that
these weapons against crime are used with discipline and restraint. It will always require good judgment and attention to the fundamental principles on
which our nation was established to insure that a
proper balance between liberty and order exists in
our nation. We must never relax our efforts to secure
that balance, because it is essential to a free society.

It is encouraging that recently in addition to criminal sanctions there is increasing attention to victims
of crime. Victims' compensation programs have been
legislated in thirty-six states to repay victims of crime
some of their lost income and medical costs. The
President's Task Force on Victims of Crime has
urged all states to set up such programs. There is also
an effort to ease the burden of the legal process itself,
which can be quite demanding on the victims it was
designed to protect.

One of the most important parts of our heritage
providing us with guidelines in our continuing
search for justice and liberty is the Bill of Rights. The
Bill of Rights withdrew the rights of the individual to
life, liberty, and property—and the fundamental
human rights as well—from the vicissitudes of political controversy and established these rights as legal
principles to be applied by our courts. These rights
do not depend on the outcome of elections but are
placed beyond the reach of legislative bodies and
government officials. The concept that there are inalienable human rights is safeguarded by a belief in
natural justice. This natural justice is universal in its
essence and causes the performance of one's legal

duty to include obedience to the urges of morality, revealed to us by the Author of Nature through the force of reason.

In discussing the subject "Natural Justice and Natural Rights," I have tried to point out that although it is the duty of the courts to follow the rules of law, this does not imply that law always fulfills our notions of the dictates of justice. Moral concern should be interwoven in the exercise of judicial justice. Morality—binding over all the globe and at all times, and resting on the foundation of a belief in and reverence for the Creator and on obedience to His will—enables man to know truth from falsehood and the just from the unjust.

The constitutional rights of life, liberty, and property are founded on principles of natural justice. Natural rights, which grow out of the nature of man, are distinguished from those which are created by positive laws enacted by a duly constituted government. Natural rights remain constant anytime and anywhere and are beyond the control of the state.

Natural justice is a sense of justice attained by the light of reason essentially agreeable with the constitution of human nature. This sense of justice has an all-important influence upon the desire to search out and apply the appropriate rules of law. It goes beyond mere technical legal rights covered by law. As Justice Oran M. Roberts described it, "it is like the polar star that guides the Voyager, although it may not stand over the port of destination."

Spinoza warned that "he who tries to fix and determine everything by law inflames rather than corrects the vices of the world." The concept of law is clouded when eternal moral principles are not understood. The history of mankind is the history of the search to discover the immediate higher law of divine origin. The moral order was revealed to man through reason, and through reason man can discern and participate in the divine plan of creation and in discovering the moral sense which dictates to him right or wrong, just or unjust. This sense may differ in degree in individual members of society, but no reasonable being, whether controlled by it or not in his conduct, is wholly destitute of it.

The Federalist, described by Jefferson as "the best commentary on the principles of government which was ever written," in its emphasis on the role of government makes the following statement: "A good government implies two things: first, fidelity to the object of government, which is happiness of the people, secondly, a knowledge of the means by which that object can be best obtained." *(Federalist 62.)* Happiness, according to *The Federalist*, requires "our safety, our tranquility, our dignity, our reputation." *(Federalist 15.)* The same requirements seem to be indispensable for a harmonious society capable of governing man's desires and passions.

Wherever the phenomenon men call their conscience or sense of justice is rooted, the just cannot be equated with the legal. Justice in the judicial sense calls for conformity to the laws that are established, but every government is a government of men and the judges who constitute the courts are also men. The courts are not wiser or better than the judges who constitute them. Furthermore, the rule of law does not sustain itself; each generation reshapes its forms and rekindles its values in the light of its own experiences.

Justice in the judicial sense, which expresses the letter of the law, is epitomized by the blindfold on the eyes of the statue emblemizing the virtue. The individual, however, must also be guided in his relations with others by the spirit of love and mercy. It is not enough to give our fellowman what is due to him. Beyond justice is the impulse of the commandment to love one another (John 13:34) and the impulse of the spirit of mercy: "And what doth the Lord require of thee, but to do justly, and to love mercy, and to walk humbly with thy God?" (Micah 6:8.)

In the Old and New Testaments, justice or the idea of righteousness calls for conformity to a standard of perfection. It signifies the possession of the virtues of faith, hope, and charity. As an attribute of God it signifies holiness; when applied to man it signifies conformity to the divine law. "Blessed are they that keep judgment, and he that doeth righteousness at all times." (Psalm 106:3.) God is the "righteous judge" (II Timothy 4:8), and "The righteousness of the law might be fulfilled in us" only if we "walk not after the flesh, but after the Spirit." (Romans 8:4.)

Dr. Barry Bailey reminds us in his lecture, "Judgment, Justice, and Mercy," that to accomplish this conformity to the divine will we must have more than an abstract desire to see that justice is done. Perfect justice is impossible because of our human limitations. Recognizing that, we must strive to attain an enlightened judgment that can take into account as many facts and conditions as possible in every circumstance. In order to transcend our own limitations and prejudices, we must make every effort to arrive at a full understanding of any situation to which we are trying to bring justice.

The outcome of such understanding is often mercy. The highest biblical injunctions command not only that justice be done but also that mercy be granted. Dr. Bailey extends the range of his discourse on justice beyond the judicial realm and brings it into the purview of all our human activities. In his view, the search for justice will bring about an attitude of compassion and a concern for the welfare of our fellowman.

Justice not only means fair conduct of the individual in his relations with others—by not violating their rights—but it also commands the individual to contribute to the common good and the welfare of the society of which he is a part. Furthermore, justice is concerned with the acts of the government and its rightful exercise of the authority necessary to maintain an orderly organized society.

The nineteenth-century British philosopher Herbert Spencer believed that harmony in a society can be obtained through the following formula of justice: "Every man is free to do that which he wills provided he infringes not the equal freedom of any other man." This formula, conformable to the belief that there is an inborn sense of justice, frees the individual from agression, protects his right to life, liberty, and the pursuit of happiness on equal terms with all, and also permits each individual—through natural selection—to prosper according to his ability and willingness to work.

The concern of justice with the welfare of society should not be confused with the variety of political thought which calls for equality in the distribution of wealth and income. In a free society, inequalities of talent, abilities, and efforts must produce inequalities in wealth, income, and status. One recent view, labeled by some as "redemptive egalitarianism," sees social justice in racial quotas, school busing, and income redistribution. Such egalitarianism is rather an expression of feelings of guilt than an enlightened commitment to justice.

The atonement for inequalities caused by rewards obtained through work and incentive does not contribute to social justice or homogeneity. Theodore H. White, interpreting the civil rights gains of the last twenty years in his recently published book *America in Search of Itself: The Making of the President 1956-1980*, points out that "one movement in the grand transformation slowly developed, year by year, into a monster whose shadow hangs over all American politics today: the division of Americans by race and national origin into groups, each entitled to special privileges." (Harper and Row, 1982, p. 129.)

Fairness consists in offering everyone equal opportunities without discrimination, but this equality cannot be obtained without the general direction of a moral code calling for service to our fellowman. Without such direction, human society becomes aimless and meaningless, and a pursuit of pleasure which weakens its spiritual fiber takes the place of the pursuit of happiness guaranteed by the Declaration of Independence. A society in which rights to

personal gratification and well-being are stressed
without correlating them with obligations to one's
fellowman and one's country cannot survive.

Mr. Ewell E. Murphy, in his lecture "Justice and
Society: Beyond Individualism," notes that the
trend of philosophical and social development since
the Renaissance—indeed since the beginning of
history—has been more and more toward the glorification of the individual, conceived of as independent of the social network around him. This triumph
of individualism has been responsible for many of
Western man's achievements in art, science, and
even religion, but it has finally gone beyond the
limits of harmony and balance. The dangers of an
excessive individualism are solipsism and a breakdown in the ties which bind society together.

Mr. Murphy observes that a retreat from the doc-
trinaire excesses of individualism has already begun,
and there is a movement toward greater emphasis on
ideas of community and cooperation. There must be
a balance between the claims of the individual and
the claims of society and of the world considered as a
whole. Only through such a search for such a social
order can we hope for peaceful solutions to the problems that besiege us.

The principle of justice which imposes moral restraints on the conduct of the individual applies to
international relations. The majesty of law pervades
the action of a nation on the international stage. One
hundred years ago, Abraham Lincoln said that this
country could not endure half slave and half free. In
the present era, we are justified in saying that this
world cannot survive in peace with one-third of its

people relatively affluent and two-thirds in misery, with unfulfilled expectations.

The demand for justice, for respect for human dignity, and for fundamental human rights throughout the world community is meaningless as long as millions of people cannot satisfy their need for sufficient food and shelter. The sooner we carry out our task of helping the people of the underdeveloped areas, the better are the hopes for a free world. Poverty, illiteracy, and ill health are the best allies of the communist aggressors.

Without minimizing the communist threat to win allegiance of underdeveloped nations, our desire for other countries to attain self-support and a decent standard of living should not be prompted only by the struggle with communist imperialism or the fear of allowing any of these nations to slip behind the Iron Curtain. The guiding spirit of our concern for less developed areas should be our commitment to help share in our fellowman's destiny. The discussion of the problem of underdeveloped areas only in the light of our struggle with communism encourages these countries to make demands on us by alerting us to their alternative of turning to communist powers.

In "Foreign Aid: Justice for Whom?" Professor W.W. Rostow surveys the history of the programs of foreign aid provided by the United States since World War II. He points out that the modern practice of sovereign governments freely offering assistance to other, less fortunate nations is wholly without precedent in the previous history of the world. To some degree, Professor Rostow notes, this bestowal

of foreign aid has been prompted by practical concerns, namely to foster international stability. But he
also points out that moral considerations—what he
calls the "missionary strand" in the American
character—have played a very large part in establish-
ing programs of foreign assistance.

Professor Rostow contends that there can be no
difference between these practical and moral
rationales. Since no country can exist alone, cut off
from the business and political relations that tie nations together, the health of one country affects all
the others. The world is one large community, and
ignoring the well-being of others imperils our own
well-being. This truth is as important in the area of
human and political rights as it is in the economic
field.

Among the basic purposes of our Constitution
listed in its Preamble is to "secure the Blessing of
Liberty to ourselves and our Posterity." This majes-
tic generality was conceived as part of the pattern of
liberal government in the eighteenth century. The
idea that liberty is attainable through mere absence
of government controls and supervision has with-
ered at least as to our economic environment, where
we can observe expanded government-imposed restraints. These changed conditions have not shaken,
however, the fundamental proposition that our government was not designed to be paternal in form. As
our courts have pointed out, we are a self-governing
people and our laws are made by us as well as for us.
The spirit of our system is to give to the individual
the utmost possible amount of personal liberty and to
let him be free to work out his destiny as his training,
desires, abilities, and talents direct him.

The spirit of a system such as ours is at total variance with that which exists in totalitarian countries. Our government was set up by the consent of the governed, and the checks and balances that exist in our system deny those in power any legal authority to coerce such consent. Through checks and balances, authority is controlled by the people, and not the people by authority. This control shines like a star in our Constitution's constellation.

Professor Kenneth W. Thompson, in his lecture "The Morality of Checks and Balances," contends that the idea of checks and balances is rooted in a profound conception of the nature of human relations. If we hold to the classic idea that man's will is flawed and that human relations cannot be expected to reach perfection, then a system of checks and balances is the only safeguard against the evils that can come of an overweaning grasp of power. All power must be under constraint, because no man or institution is good enough to enjoy untrammeled power.

The wisdom of this view of human nature can be seen not only in the American constitutional system, into which a system of checks and balances was built by design, but also on the international stage, where a balance of power—fragile as it may be—is the best safeguard against aggression we have yet discovered. A realist view may not be as appealing as one that predicates the possibility of the perfection of human nature and human society. But we have only to look at societies which fraudulently attempt to claim perfection—which is the basis of the communist system—to see what peril lies in that direction. Human rights and human dignity must be protected from those who would wield absolute power by means of some independent spiritual and moral source.

The 1982 Lectures on Moral Values in a Free Society convince us that there is no loftier responsibility than to uphold the principles of justice that protect us from aggression which infringes on the natural rights of the citizen. These rights are not derived from any Constitution; they existed anterior to the Constitution. In searching for justice, we search for the means to enjoy those unalienable rights with which our Creator endowed us. The faith in the dignity and worth of every individual is the underlying philosophy of life that gives coherence and the proper direction to our thoughts and actions.

LIBERTY AND JUSTICE FOR ALL: KEEPING THE SCALES IN BALANCE

by

William H. Webster

William H. Webster

Judge Webster has served as Director of the Federal Bureau of Investigation since 1978. He was awarded a Bacheolor of Arts degree from Amherst College in 1947, and in 1975 that institution bestowed on him an honorary Doctor of Laws degree. He received his Juris Doctor degree from Washington University Law School in 1949.

A practicing attorney with a St. Louis, Missouri, law firm from 1949 to 1959, Judge Webster served as United States Attorney for the Eastern District of Missouri from 1960 to 1961. From 1964 to 1969, he was a member of the Missouri Board of Law Examiners.

In 1970, Judge Webster was appointed Judge of the United States District Court for the Eastern District of Missouri and in 1973 was elevated to the United States Court of Appeals for the Eighth Circuit. During his service on the bench, he was Chairman of the Judicial Conference Advisory Committee on the Criminal Rules and was a member of the Ad Hoc Committee on Habeas Corpus and the Committee of Court Administration.

Judge Webster served as Chairman of the Corporation, Banking and Business Law Section of the American Bar Association, and is a fellow of the American Bar Foundation. In 1972 he received a Washington University Alumni Citation for contributions to the field of law, and in 1977 he received the Distinguished Alumnus Award from Washington University Law School. He is a member of the Board of Trustees of Washington University.

Judge Webster holds honorary degrees from eleven colleges and universities. He was named Man of the Year, 1980, by the St. Louis Globe-Democrat, and in May 1981 he received the William Greenleaf Elliott Award from Washington University and the Riot Relief Fund award from New York. He was elected a member of the Academy of Missouri Squires in 1981.

LIBERTY AND JUSTICE FOR ALL:
KEEPING THE SCALES IN BALANCE

by

William H. Webster

It is a great pleasure for me to be here in Dallas and to participate in this lecture series. The search for justice is a challenging and interesting subject, and I am happy to be included in the overall project of Dr. Cecil to reflect on moral values in a free society, particularly in the series on justice.

I would like to begin with an incident that occurred in my life and influenced some of my thinking. I had served as a naval officer in World War II, had returned to law school, and had been in practice for about a year when I was recalled to active duty during the Korean War. When I reported as executive officer of a naval tanker at Pearl Harbor, the ship was being prepared for a trip to the Far East. One night I came back on board, and the Captain was looking for me. He said, "They've had a little bit of trouble, and I wish that you would see if you could help some of our crew." I was the only lawyer on board and a pretty young one at that. Two of our crew members had been taken off the ship by military police and were being questioned as suspects in an attempted theft of an automobile car battery from one of the dock workers in the shipyard.

I went to the Navy Yard at Pearl Harbor where the questioning was taking place, and I asked to see the men. I was told, "Well, they're being questioned." I replied, "I know. That's why I'd like to talk to them." After a while they did let me see the men, and I said, "I would just like to know whether you have advised these men that they do not have to answer questions?" Somebody there said, "Well, we told them that they had certain constitutional rights." I asked, "Did you mention that among those rights is the right not to answer questions?" "Well, no." "Well, let me just tell my men that they have that right."

I will not extend the story much further. Actually, the men did cooperate, at least by my standards they did. We sailed for Japan and Korea, and several weeks later a letter came to the ship from the Admiral who was the Commandant of the 14th Naval District. In summary it said, "Due to Lieutenant Webster's interference, we were unable to obtain a conviction." My Captain said, "Here, you write the response and I'll sign it." In my official response, I pointed out that even naval courts and boards recognize the right that I was espousing. Moreover, the proposed Uniform Code of Military Justice, which would be adopted within months of this time, had the same provisions. I also stated that there was a presumption of innocence that seemed to be ignored in their statement that due to my interference they had been unable to obtain a confession.

After this reply, a very restless Lieutenant was in the Far East waiting to see what might happen to his future. But the bottom line of the response was, I am happy to say, that Lieutenant Webster in representing his men had done no more than to secure for them the rights guaranteed to them by the Constitution of the United States. No further action was contemplated.

That incident antedated *Gideon v. Wainright, Escobedo v. Illinois* (which was very close on its facts), and the *Miranda* decision. But this was our Constitution in action. Involved was the presumption of innocence: vindicated. Involved was the right to counsel: vindicated. And involved was the right not to be a witness against oneself: vindicated. And it was clear that these rights applied to any person subject to prosecution under the law of the United States, any place, any time.

I would like to say at the beginning of this lecture that those of us charged with the enforcement of our laws accept and support these rights. After all, they protect us too. It is in the Bill of Rights that individual liberties are enshrined. In more modern times, we have added the concept of privacy rights—not specifically defined in the Constitution, but perceived and acknowledged by the Supreme Court as being within the penumbra of the Bill of Rights. These individual liberties and privacy interests, sometimes called the right to be "let alone," have become important and cherished values in our society.

Despite this strong tradition, there are other voices to be reckoned with. These are the voices of a collective society, heard most often when individuals in the exercise of their own liberties intrude upon the rights of others, or where crime and fear of crime evoke the cry: "Do something about it. We have a right to be safe and free." All of us who have roles in the administration of justice are confronted by these two apparently competing values—both deeply treasured by us all.

This challenge is not new. Even at the time the American Revolution was brewing, Edmund Burke defined his sense of liberty with these words:

"The only liberty that is valuable is a liberty connected with order; that not only exists with order and virtue, but which cannot exist at all without them."

Rather than focus upon liberty and order, I would rather shift your view slightly to liberty and justice for all: keeping the scales in balance.

Daniel Webster said that "justice is the great interest of man on earth."

Few would dispute this statement. I passionately believe it to be true. But this only gives us a concept. Justice for whom? What is justice? Throughout recorded history we find attempts to define it, such as Justinian's "Justice is the firm and continuous desire to render to everyone that which is his due." I think that a workable definition is that justice is the moral signification of law. But in fashioning justice, do we focus upon the accused, upon the victim, or upon society? Keeping the scales in balance is not an easy undertaking, but it is a noble one and one worthy of our best talents and energy.

I have come to the conclusion that the essence of justice is fairness judged by contemporary standards. Both the law and the process by which the law is adjudicated must satisfy our standard of justice and, equally important, the appearance of justice. Justice must not only be done but must be seen to be done. But simply being fair to the accused is not the full answer. Fairness implicates not only the accused but also the victim and, indeed, all of us.

Many of the rights and privileges we enjoy in this society of ours were not available at all, or in comparable degree, when our Constitution was ratified by the original states. All these changes have come about without changing a word in the Bill of Rights. The Supreme Court has interpreted a living document to conform to its understanding of emerging standards of decency. Certainly, this has been the case in defining the application of the prohibition against cruel and unusual punishment. It has been true also in interpreting the due process clause to make clear how much process is due.

In the balancing process, the courts often seek to protect the sanctity of the courts as well as to enforce compliance with constitutional requirements. For example, in the mid-1900s, the Supreme Court determined that evidence obtained in violation of constitutional provisions should be excluded from the trial, not because the evidence was false or unreliable but to deter future misconduct by law enforcement officers. This approach, which has withstood attack in the courts for over half a century, has not been without its vigorous critics. Justice Cardozo exclaimed in disapproval that "the prisoner must go free because the Constable has blundered." Our present Chief Justice has pointed out in numerous opinions, most notably in his decision in the *Bivans* case, that the *mechanical application* of the exclusionary rule was undercutting confidence in the justice system. I agree with the observation.

Currently, the Admininistration has proposed a legislative modification of the exclusionary rule, in which a reasonable good-faith belief by the officer that his conduct was lawful would avoid the automatic application of the exclusionary rule. Proponents of the rule argue that there are not enough cases involving the exclusionary rule to make much difference in the crime rate. I think the problem cuts much deeper than that. It goes to whether or not the scales have been unfairly tilted in favor of the accused and against society. I suspect that a majority of citizens concerned about crime believe that this has happened. The legislative initiative is at least one approach to putting the scales in balance.

Not all court-decreed restrictions on law enforcement are harmful to a popular sense of fairness. Critics of the *Miranda* rule, for example, have not convinced me that crime would drop or our system of justice would be improved by its abolition. The FBI had been giving *Miranda* warnings—principally the right to remain silent and the right to counsel—to suspects in custodial settings for more than twenty years before the *Miranda* case was decided, with no noticeable impediment to our investigations.

In the balancing process, those of us who have been entrusted with the enforcement of the law must often move through mine fields as we attempt to understand and apply what has been determined by the courts and to anticipate the responses to future issues. Tests of reasonableness, reasonable belief, and good faith are always applied after the fact, and many a police officer has wished that he might have had the benefit of twenty-twenty hindsight. If, however, the law enforcement agency trains and advises its officers promptly and clearly when new rules are announced or old ones clarified, the lessons will be learned, and they will be incorporated into current and future practice. That is, provided the lessons are clear enough to be understood. The law of search and seizure, for example, is in a state of disarray. In my view, the police officer on the beat with very little time to inquire needs a clearer guide than is now available to him when on short notice he must make important decisions.

One example of keeping law enforcement officers informed is the practice that we apply in the Bureau. When I came on board, I directed that within forty-eight hours of any major change in the law in any Circuit in the United States the Bureau inform the Agents serving within that Circuit and follow up with additional training and information.

The *Dalia* case is a good example of these procedures. The Sixth Circuit, headquartered in Cincinnati, ruled that in connection with court-authorized wiretaps the Congress had not given in Title III, and could not give to the courts, the power to authorize a surreptitious entry in order to install a court-authorized microphone. It seemed to me this was not a very sensible ruling. Are our Agents supposed to knock on the door and say, "Sir, may I come in and place a hidden microphone the court has authorized in your building?" However, that was the ruling. Within forty-eight hours, our Agents within the Sixth Circuit, primarily the North Central States, were informed that all Title III microphone installations that were in place at that time should be discontinued.

Not long after that, the Ninth Circuit on the West Coast followed with a similar ruling and the same process occurred. Finally in the Third Circuit, headquartered in Philadelphia, a case reached that court and then went to the Supreme Court. The Supreme Court held that the authority to make the entry was implied. The implication was so obvious it was not even necessary for that authority to be contained in the court order itself. Back to the field we went, reinstating the court-authorized electronic surveillances that we had terminated in the Sixth Circuit and in the Ninth Circuit.

But I added one other requirement. Notwithstanding the Supreme Court, we would continue to request the judges before whom we appeared for court-authorized wiretaps to specifically acknowledge that we had authority to make those entries. I wanted to build a record against a future time when some other question could be raised about it, and also to make sure that the judge did, in fact, understand that we intended and had to make a surreptitious entry in order to put that microphone in place. There are still a few judges who say, "Why do you do this when the Supreme Court doesn't require you to do it?" But I think it makes sense, and it illustrates the discipline that we impose upon ourselves to be sure that our conduct conforms with the latest changes and shifts in the law.

Those to whom the enforcement of the laws is entrusted must have the authority and the power necessary to compel obedience from those who refuse to play by the rules established in a free society. But this is not an unbridled authority. It is circumscribed by the probable cause requirement of the Constitution in arrest situations, a reasonable suspicion test which can be articulated in a stop and frisk situation, and both probable cause and a test of reasonableness in search and seizure cases. The warrant requirement interposes the judgment of a neutral magistrate in many of these situations. This protects the citizen under suspicion. Usually, in exigent circumstances the warrant requirement may be waived, but later the emergency needs are subject to review. This protects both the subject of the investigation and the public. In other words, there is a sense of fairness about it.

For over a decade lawyers and philosophers have been arguing about how much force can be utilized by law enforcement officers. We are told to use reasonable force to subdue a person who resists the exercise of lawful authority. In tight situations that may include the use of deadly force. But what are the outer limits of that point? When is the use of that force so excessive that it cannot be countenanced in a free society?

I suppose that the issue is most apparent in the case of a fatal shooting of a fleeing suspect. A petty thief may face a few months or years in jail if caught; but because he elects to flee or simply flees from fear, he may be executed in the process of compelling him to stop. Clearly the police officer should not have to win a foot race to establish his authority; equally clear, the dangerousness of the situation must be assessed before he uses deadly force.

In the FBI, we train our Agents only to use their weapons to protect themselves or others from injury or where the suspect has first used deadly force himself. It is a "protect life" standard, and it is built into our discipline; it serves us and the country well. Many states are now legislating similar requirements.

I use this example not only because it is an important illustration of the competing values I have been discussing but also because it shows the emphasis our society often places on legislative or judicial solutions. In my view, there will be few cases where the trier of fact will want to substitute his judgment for that of an officer in a clear emergency. That we have left so difficult a choice to the officer may reflect our preoccupation with legal formulations, when we have failed to provide the officer with a *weapons* solution. If we can put a man on the moon, it seems to me we can develop an alternative weapon for a police officer which, in nondangerous situations, can be used to stop but not kill. Surely this would serve the interests both of individual rights and the needs of the public as a whole. I have urged this from time to time, not as a substitute weapon but as an alternative weapon to be carried by police officers, and I truly believe that it would answer the question without trying judicial or legislative solutions. Thus far there has been inadequate interest in really developing a workable weapon.

Perhaps you will recall the concerns expressed about a dozen years ago when in the wake of numerous skyjackings the FAA and the airlines took action to require inspection of baggage and passengers boarding airplanes. Others, however, viewed these inspection stops as intrusive, offensive, and a step toward "1984." Well, as the year 1984 actually approaches, it seems to me we have survived these concerns. The X-ray machines speed the process and minimize the sense of invasion of privacy. The metal detectors are simple and inoffensive. We have learned to subordinate our own turf-consciousness to assure a larger measure of safety to all the passengers who share the plane with us.

I venture to say that any proposal today to eliminate these precautions would be met by a storm of protest. This is another good lesson in striking the balance to achieve fairness.

The process by which these values are accommodated proceeds at many levels—the Constitution, statutes, regulations or guidelines, and occasionally technological solutions. The examples I have given serve, all too briefly, to illustrate the interplay of values at these levels.

Sometimes the demands made upon a criminal justice system are very heavy, and it is in such times that the balance comes under greatest stress. This is true today. There are not enough law enforcement officers, not enough prosecutors, not enough judges, and not enough prisons and probation officers to deal with those who refuse to play by our rules. We rarely deal with these problems systematically. Each effort to improve one component of the system is very apt to place the others in imbalance. It takes five years to construct a federal penal institution, yet prisons tend to be the last components to be assessed, and usually after some judge has ruled that an institution is unconstitutionally overcrowded and inhumane.

Our crime record reached an all time high in 1980, an increase of 22 percent since 1977. During 1981, it leveled off, and in the first six months of 1982 we experienced our first slight decline since 1975. This is small comfort when our bench mark is the highest crime rate in our history.

Despite an ever increasing level of professionalism, our numbers have sagged as inflation eroded our capacity to keep an adequate number of law enforcement officers on the rolls. I believe the number of police officers in New York has been cut by approximately one-third. Since 1976 the FBI has lost over 800 Agents.

Our reluctance to seek finality in the courts has opened up endless avenues of collateral attack which further compound an already congested and overtaxed machinery. Most recently, where undercover techniques have been employed by the government, we have seen due process hearings, both before and after trial, added to the arsenal of defense procedures. One judge has predicted to me that these lengthy procedures will become routine whenever an undercover agent is utilized in an investigation. Many of these hearings seem to be an effort to retry specific defenses already rejected by the jury. Indeed, so much of our administrative effort is involved in anticipating and dealing with such collateral attacks that our documentation may soon rival the defensive medicine now practiced by some physicians. Occasionally, one is reminded of Judge Henry Friendly's plaintive question some years ago: "Is innocence irrelevant?"

Still we are accountable, must be accountable, and must always be prepared to demonstrate that our investigations are conducted within the rule of law.

And what challenges! In the past four and one half years I have seen our agency called upon to deal with increasing efforts of hostile intelligence services to steal our precious technology; evict Iranian and Libyan diplomatic establishments and provide crucial intelligence during those trying times; investigate skyjackings; wrap up international terrorist groups operating in our country; resolve hostage situations; conduct civil rights investigations; investigate the shooting of a President; assist local law enforcement authorities in local tragedies of national importance—Atlanta, Buffalo, Fort Wayne, and now Chicago; find the murderers of a federal judge; assist foreign countries such as Italy and El Salvador; provide disaster assistance in air crashes and in Jonestown; launch a major assault on organized crime to reach beyond the streets into the upper echelons of major criminal enterprises; and find ways to bring to account those public officials who betray their trust. That is a big order for 7,800 Agents.

Modern technology has put at our fingertips techniques which materially advance our ability to gather information with which to discharge our law enforcement responsibilities. Electronic surveillance, video tapes, the computer, lasers, all these and more are integrated into our arsenal against crime and espionage. They carry great potential for good and a corresponding potential for abuse.

The answer is at least in part in two areas—first, in defining the rules by which these techniques may be used; and second, in a level of accountability that assures the public and those in authority that the techniques are being utilized according to the rules.

The same is true when we talk about undercover work. This technique has proved to be enormously effective in reaching those predisposed to engage in consensual crimes, sometimes called "victimless" crimes—narcotics, gambling, prostitution and bribery. (Of course, there is really no such thing as a victimless crime—we citizens are the victims of these practices, especially by those who betray the offices entrusted to them.)

Because the technique may be said to be intrusive, we subject the undercover process to close internal scrutiny, including an undercover activity review committee with representatives from the Department of Justice. The ongoing effort, carried out in compliance with Attorney General guidelines, serves to safeguard those under suspicion from entrapment and government overreaching, and at the same time helps us protect the public from corrupt officials and organized criminal enterprises with extensive layers of insulation.

We are now engaged in what may prove the greatest challenge to law enforcement—a major concerted effort to halt the heavy cost in crime and human lives generated by those who traffic in illegal drugs and narcotics. Once again our target is the criminal enterprise. But this time the dollars involved are so great that we must confront arrogance and corrupting capacity unparalleled in our history.

We must keep the scales in balance. I think the procedures, the discipline, and the guidance we are receiving are designed to improve our effectiveness within the rule of law.

But procedures and accounting alone will not suffice. Among the moral values at play here is integrity. I think we need to be reminded of the words of Sir William Stephenson, known to many as the "Man Called Intrepid," who wrote:

> "Among the increasingly intricate arsenals across the world, intelligence is an essential weapon, perhaps the most important. But it is being secret, the most dangerous. Safeguards to prevent its abuse must be devised, revised, and rigidly applied. But, as in all enterprises, the character and wisdom of those to whom it is entrusted will be decisive. In the integrity of that guardianship lies the hope of free people to endure and prevail."

He was, of course, speaking of intelligence. But I think what he said applies equally to all who enforce the laws and shape the balance that Edmund Burke called liberty with order and virtue.

Margaret Chase Smith, the distinguished former Senator from Maine, once commented upon the problem of forced choice during the years of dissent in the 1960s. She said that most Americans, if forced to choose between anarchy and repression, would reluctantly choose repression. That choice must never be thrust upon us. We have the means to strive for justice by a justice system which fairly takes into account the rights of the individual and the needs of society and the victims of crime. It is an ongoing task, and one which I dare say is too important to be left entirely to lawyers. Justice belongs to all our citizens. We must work at it, work to keep the machinery functioning, work to keep our societal standards decent and high, work to instill in our children a clearer

vision of justice—one which functions both for individuals and for society because it is fair. We must
strike that balance true, because in our ability to
keep the scales in balance lies our future as a land of
ordered liberty.

NATURAL JUSTICE AND NATURAL RIGHTS

by

Andrew R. Cecil

Andrew R. Cecil

Dr. Cecil is Chancellor Emeritus and Trustee of The Southwestern Legal Foundation and Distinguished Scholar in Residence at The University of Texas at Dallas.

Associated with the Foundation since 1958, Dr. Cecil has helped guide its development of five educational centers that offer nationally and internationally recognized programs in advanced continuing education.

In February 1979 the University established in his honor the Andrew R. Cecil Lectures on Moral Values in a Free Society, and invited Dr. Cecil to deliver the first series of lectures in November 1979. The first annual proceedings were published as Dr. Cecil's book The Third Way: Enlightened Capitalism and the Search for a New Social Order, *which received an enthusiastic response. He also lectured in the 1980 and 1981 series.*

Educated in Europe and well launched on a career as a professor and practitioner in the fields of law and economics, Dr. Cecil resumed his academic career after World War II in Lima, Peru, at the University of San Marcos. After 1949, he was associated with the Methodist church-affiliated colleges and universities in the United States until he joined the Foundation. He is author of twelve books on the subjects of law and economics and of more than seventy articles on these subjects and on the philosophy of religion published in periodicals and anthologies.

A member of the American Society of International Law, of the American Branch of the International Law Association, and of the American Judicature Society, Dr. Cecil has served on numerous commissions for the Methodist Church, and is a member of the Board of Trustees of the National Methodist Foundation for Christian Higher Education. Dr. Cecil also serves as a member of the Development Board of The University of Texas at Dallas. In 1981 he was named an Honorary Rotarian.

NATURAL JUSTICE AND NATURAL RIGHTS

by

Andrew R. Cecil

What Kind of Virtue?

The battle cry of the French Revolution was *Liberté, egalité, fraternité.* The maxim of the American Revolution was "Taxation without representation is tyranny." In the nineteenth century, the slogan of the Polish patriots in their struggle against Czarist Russia was "For your freedom and ours." Later this slogan was adopted by progressive democratic world leaders, who identified it with the course of liberty. In Russia itself in 1917, the Bolsheviks sought a "dictatorship of the proletariat," and their slogan sounded everywhere: "Peace to the army, land to the peasants, control of the factories to the workers."

All these rallying cries prompt us to ask why, in times of turmoil and tension, when people demand the rectification of errors and atrocities, they place the highest values on freedom, brotherhood, and equality in the distribution of wealth and of opportunity, without mentioning justice as one of the moral, spiritual, economic, or political aims to be achieved.

What kind of a virtue is justice? Epicurus finds that "justice never is anything in itself" but is "a kind of compact not to harm or be harmed" in our dealings

with one another. Saint Augustine believes that we
are in the midst of evils which cannot be removed
from our life either by justice, prudence, or temperance, unless these virtues are used in service to God,
for there is in man "a certain just order of nature, so
that the soul is subjected to God, and the flesh to the
soul, and consequently both soul and flesh to God
. . ." There is no justice nor any other true virtue,
states Augustine, where there is no religion.

Aristotle in his *Nichomachean Ethics*, admitting
the ambiguity of the terms "justice" and "injustice,"
concludes that justice is "not part of virtue but virtue
entire," that it is "often thought to be the greatest of
virtues," and that "neither evening nor morning star
is so wonderful." It is, he believes, the complete
virtue in its fullest sense, because he who possesses
it can exercise his virtue not only in himself but
toward his neighbor also. The importance of justice
in the relationship with other persons is also stressed
in Artistotle's discussion of friendship, the virtue
"most indispensable for life." When people are
friends, he writes, "they have no need of justice, but
when they are just, they need friendship in addition.
In fact, the just in the fullest sense is regarded as
constituting an element of friendship."

To Plato a just society is a perfect society. As the
effective "harmony of the whole," justice is the
supreme, overarching virtue. It does not permit the
several elements within man "to interfere with one
another." Justice binds the three principles involved
in moral behavior. These principles or basic elements, according to Plato, are: (1) wisdom, which
governs the soul by reason; (2) temperance, which

calls for the rational regulation of our desires or appetites; and (3) courage, the spirit which retains and enforces "the commands of reason" about what we ought or ought not to do.

The harmony of these three faculties constitutes justice. When this harmonious condition is achieved, the just man "sets in order his own inner life, and is his own master and his own law, and at peace with himself." When strife arises among the three principles, injustice occurs—the "rising up of a part of the soul against the whole," creating confusion and disease, which destroy the natural order of the personality. Justice, states Plato, is an institution of natural order, and injustice creates things "at variance with the natural order."

In the Old and New Testaments, justice is identified with the very essence of divinity. The invocation of divine justice signifies not a request to satisfy a claim but a request for grace: "Hear my prayer, O Lord, give ear to my supplications: in thy faithfulness answer me, and in thy righteousness." (Psalm 143:1.) Moses describes the Lord as "a God of truth and without iniquity, just and right is He." (Deuteronomy 32:4.) As St. Thomas expressed it: *cum ipse sit jus justicia* ("The justice of God is inherent in Himself"). There is, therefore, a distinction between divine justice and human justice. Divine justice, of a metaphysical character, represents God's will, in which justice—which comprises the gift of grace—is fused with pity, goodness, and wisdom. Human justice calls for conformity to the divine will. In the words of the Gospel, "Blessed are they which do hunger and thirst after righteousness; for they shall be filled." (Matthew 5:6.)

A Word of Many Meanings

The definitions of justice are so various that it is unsatisfactory to single out one. The meaning of the word cannot be defined with precision. It is sufficient to say that the end of justice is to protect our natural and civil rights in our relations to other individuals, to our society, and to the state. Justice rectifies the errors we commit when we transgress the allowed limits of our natural rights, or violate man-made laws, or exercise the powers of government arbitrarily. Because of the restraint imposed by natural justice upon the various natural inalienable rights, we have to acknowledge the primacy of justice as the supreme value.

Discussion of the various kinds of justice reveals conflict and confusion, because justice is a word of many meanings. Among the numerous definitions of distinct kinds of justice, we shall list some of the more important ones. Aristotle originated the distinction between distributive and commutative (rectificatory) justice. The first one governs the distribution of rewards and punishments to each according to his merits and services. Since it does not consider all men equal, distributive justice discriminates between them by observing a just proportion and comparison so that neither equal persons have unequal things nor unequal persons equal things. Commutative justice governs contracts and is based on equality between the parties. Its object is to render to everyone what belongs to him without regard to his personal worth or merits, so that no one gains by another's loss.

Pufendorf—the German jurist, statesman, and historian (1632-1694)—divides justice into imperfect or universal and perfect or particular. The first discharges duties that cannot be exacted by the law; the latter deals with duties strictly demanded by law. The French jurist Toullier (1752-1835) prefers the division of internal and external justice as the only division "clear, exact, and useful" *(La division de la justice en intérieure ou extérieure nous parait la seule claire, la seule exacte, la seule utile)*. Internal justice, he states, conforms to our will and is the object of morality; external deals with our actions and is the object of jurisprudence. The medieval French jurist A. Michel held the opinion that all kinds of justice—whether distributive, commutative, or legal—are social justice, since they concern the relation between man and man.

The list of suggested divisions of justice could be continued, but it seems that we have reached the point of realization that we must use the term "justice" carefully and limit our discussion to only one of its aspects. For this reason, our comments will be devoted to the idea of natural justice and one of its great purposes—the preservation of natural, fundamental rights, which should be sacred.

Natural justice, according to our courts, is founded "in equity, in honesty and right." It dictates that we should do what is "fair." That which is fair, the courts have stated, "is a question of standards of conduct, about which men may differ." Natural justice, like natural law, is revealed to us by the light of reason and remains in essential agreement with the constitution of human nature. According to some philosophers, it is the judgment based on the eternal rule of righteousness which God inscribed upon the heart of every man, which enables us to know truth from falsehood and good from evil. President Calvin Coolidge referred to that eternal character of law when he announced that "men do not make laws, they do but discover them."

When we accept the premise of the existence of an ethical imperative, we have to answer the question whether there exists an interdependence of law, justice, and morals. For Calvin, the moral law "prescribed to men of all ages and natures" is identical with a declaration of natural law. "This equity," he wrote, "must alone be the scope, and rule, and end, of all laws." Thomas Aquinas argued that "tyrannical law, not being according to reason, is not law at all in the true and strict sense but is a perversion of law." Saint Augustine offers the far-reaching conclusion that "that which is not just seems to be no law at all." Martin Luther rejected the whole body of canon law, which governed the medieval church and by which the church sought to govern society in general. In December of the year 1520, he staged a bookburning on the bank of the Elbe; into the flames went the whole library of canon law, which, according to Luther, "has arisen in the devil's name."

Equity Law

Equity law owes its existence to this same sense of discrepancy between the law as it exists and the law as it ought to be. It arose from the defectiveness of human laws and their inability to remedy their own deficiencies or to moderate their harshness when applied to a particular case. Grotius defined equity as *Correctrix eius in quo lex propter universalitatem deficit* ("the correction of that in which the law is lacking because of its very universality"). The principle of equity was known as early as the Roman period. The Roman praetors held the first courts of equity, and the *jus praetorium* was a collection of rules introduced by the praetors to protect the citizens from the iniquitous operation of municipal law.

From Rome this practice was transplanted to almost every civilized nation. In some countries the king, in others a special counsel, reviewed the decisions of the courts when a party could not obtain justice through ordinary channels or sought moderation of the rigors of the law when applied to an individual case. With the growth of civilization and the extension of commerce, the equity courts accommodated their jurisdiction to these growing exigencies, thus gaining strength as time went on. When the existing law did not respond to changes and its settled principles operated inadequately, the natural result was a search for new avenues to express the moral element which permeates the judicial process.

There is no agreement among the American legal giants, or at least there is uncertainty on the part of the Supreme Court, as to whether law and morals are separate modes of social control or whether they are to be made identical by conforming the existing legal precepts to the requirements of a reasoned system of morals. Justice Benjamin Cardozo in his *Paradoxes of Legal Science* stressed the need for a judge to respond to a "moral urge" and claimed that as a result of such a response "the moral norm and the jural have been brought together, and are one." Whenever a conflict exists, Cardozo held, "moral values are to be preferred to economic, and economic to aesthetic." (Columbia University Press, 1928, pp. 46, 57.)

While the British Chief Justice Lord Mansfield elaborated extensively on the need to inject moral concepts into the law, another illustrious legal reformer, Jeremy Bentham, believed that such concepts as natural rights and natural justice prove "two things only, the heat of passion, and the darkness of understanding." He asserted that the only test of the goodness or badness of a law is its actual effect on human beings, their pain, and their pleasure.

In Germany, Friedrich Karl von Savigny (1779-1861), one of the foremost jurists of his age, was one of the earliest adherents of the historical school of jurisprudence. He resisted the imposition of legal codes and denied the efficacy of legal reform alien to the people it has to serve. What binds people, states Savigny, "is the common conviction of the people, the kindred consciousness of an inward necessity, *excluding all notion of an accidental and arbitrary origin.* [Emphasis added.]" In other words, Savigny saw in historic experience a substitute for the standard of reason, with no need of conformity to an *a priori* principle of right or just law such as that offered by the doctrine of natural law and justice.

The essence of Savigny's idea was expressed by Justice Oliver Wendell Holmes when he wrote in his *The Common Law:*

"The life of the law has not been logic: it has been experience. The felt necessities of the time, the prevalent moral and political theories, intuitions of public policy, avowed or unconscious, even the prejudices which judges share with their fellow-men have had a good deal more to do than the syllogism in determining the rules by which men should be governed."

In the United States, Justices Holmes and Felix Frankfurter were among the most illustrious and outspoken jurists who believed that moral and ethical values should not be injected into the law. They opposed any attempt on the part of judges to make the law conform to an ideal moral standard. Justice Frankfurter, dissenting in the case of *West Virginia Board of Education v. Barnette,* wrote that it can never be emphasized too much "that one's opinion about the wisdom or evil of a law should be excluded altogether when one is doing one's duty on the bench." (319 U.S. 624, 647, 63 S. Ct. 1178, 1189 [1943].)

Justice Holmes, skeptical as to our knowledge "of the goodness or badness of laws," held that a judge's responsibility is to enforce in good faith and to the best of his ability "whatever constitutional laws Congress or anybody sees fit to pass." His decisions, for instance, enforced antitrust laws, although as a believer in the theory of the survival of the strong he viewed the Sherman Act as one based on economic incompetence and ignorance. As reported by Francis Biddle, a former Attorney General of the United States, Justice Holmes exclaimed in a conversation with John Davis, the Solicitor General of the United States, after trying an antitrust case: "Of course I know, and every other sensible man knows, that the Sherman law is damned nonsense, but if my country wants to go to hell, I am here to help it." (*Justice Holmes, Natural Law, and the Supreme Court*, The Macmillan Company, 1961, p. 9.) He believed that "law, being a practical thing, must found itself on actual forces."

Holmes rejected the concept of abstract justice when he wrote "that the Common Law is not a brooding omnipresence in the sky and the U.S. is not subject to some mystic overlaw that it is bound to obey." The difference between abstract justice and the law was also described in forceful terms by Justice Oran M. Roberts of the Supreme Court of Texas, one of the greatest judges the state has ever had. (He was also Governor of Texas at the time The University of Texas was established.) He defines justice as "a dictate of right, according to the common consent of mankind generally or of that portion of mankind who may be governed by the same principles and morals." It represents, he believes, "a chaotic mass of principles," while law classifies and reduces to order the same mass of principles and puts them in the shape of rules agreed upon by common consent.

Justice, states Roberts, "is the virgin gold of the mines, that passes for its intrinsic worth in every case, but is subject to varying value, according to the scales through which it passes. Law is the coin from the mint, with its value ascertained and fixed, with the stamp of government upon it which assures and denotes its value." Concludes Justice Roberts, "To follow the dictates of justice, when in harmony with the law, must be a pleasure; but to follow the rules of law, in their true spirit, to whatever consequences they may lead, is a duty."

Courts and Legislatures

Judges are not at liberty to substitute their own ideas for the wishes of legislators. They cannot substitute their social, political, and economic beliefs for the judgment of legislative bodies, which are elected to pass laws. "It must be remembered that legislatures are ultimate guardians of the liberties and welfare of the people in quite as great degree as courts." (*Missouri, K & T Co. v. May,* 194 U.S. 267, 270, 24 S.CT. 638, 639 [1904].)

Justice in the judicial sense calls for exact conformity to obligatory law. Judicial power can be exercised only for the purpose of giving effect to the will of the law and not to the will of the judge. Judicial discretion is a legal discretion to be exercised according to known and established rules, not an arbitrary power of the judge. The English statesman and philosopher Francis Bacon wrote in 1625: "Judges ought to remember that their office is to interpret law and not to make or give law." Montesquieu believed that "the judges of the nation are only the mouths that pronounce the words of the law, inanimate beings, who can moderate neither its force nor its rigor." Chief Justice Marshall stressed that "judicial power is never exercised for the purpose of giving effect to the will of the judge; always for the purpose of giving effect to the will of the legislature; or in other words, to the will of the law." (*Osborn v. Bank of the United States*, 9 Wheat. 738, 866 [1824].) History gives ample evidence that mankind benefits more from an administration of justice where rights are determined by a system of rules rather than by a sense of abstract justice as conceived by the judge.

To follow the rules of law is the duty of the court, which is a mere instrument of the law. This does not imply that law always fulfills our notions of the dictates of justice. There are moral claims and duties, comprehended under humanity, benevolence, or charity, which law does not enforce; their fulfillment is left to man's conscience and honor. Law is not always accepted as moral by an enlightened public opinion nor does it always punish or restrain some of the violations of our moral sense.

The history of jurisprudence gives ample evidence that law cannot be separated from moral values. There are numerous reasons why moral concern is interwoven in the exercise of judicial justice. The nature of the judicial process, as projected by President Theodore Roosevelt in his message to the Congress of the United States of December 8, 1908, met with severe criticism on the part of those who believed that the only authority of a judge is to follow the rule of law. In that message President Roosevelt declared:

> "The chief lawmakers in our country may be, and often are, the judges, because they are the final seal of authority. Every time they interpret contract, property, vested rights, due process of law, liberty, they necessarily enact into law parts of a

system of social philosophy; and such interpretation is fundamental, they give direction to all lawmaking. The decisions of the courts on economic and social questions depend upon their economic and social philosophy; and for the peaceful progress of our people during the twentieth century we shall owe most to those judges who hold to a twentieth century economic and social philosophy and not to a long outgrown philosophy, which was itself the product of primitive economic conditions."

Changing Views

The changes that constantly occur in our dynamic society—economic, social, and political—create new demands which have an impact on the courts' reasoning. Because of these demands, the principle of adhering to precedent—which offers continuity with the past and attempts to guarantee that all people will be treated alike—no longer satisfies our society's expectation that the judicial process can be adapted to varying conditions. The Supreme Court of the United States has explicitly asserted its right to overrule a prior constitutional decision when it realizes that the prior principle is wrong. The Court has stated that it feels justified in having more freedom to overrule prior constitutional decisions than to change its interpretations of other laws, since the Constitution is difficult to amend, while mere statutes or other legal principles which do not raise constitutional issues can easily be changed by legislative action. (*Smith v. Allwright,* 321 U.S. 649, 665 [1944].)

With respect to segregated schools, for instance, the courts adhered for over half a century to the doctrine of "separate but equal" that appeared in 1896 in the United States Supreme Court ruling on the case of *Plessy v. Ferguson.* (163 U.S. 537 [1896].) Under that doctrine, equality of treatment is accorded when the races are provided substantially equal facilities, even though these facilities be separate. Over fifty years later, in 1954 in the case of *Brown v. Board of Education of Topeka,* the Supreme Court held that segregation of children in public schools solely on the basis of race, even though the physical facilities and other tangible factors may be equal, deprives the children of the minority group of equal educational opportunities in contravention of the Equal Protection Clause of the Fourteenth Amendment. The Court concluded that in the field of public education the doctrine of "separate but equal" has no place, because "we cannot turn the clock . . . to 1896 when *Plessy v. Ferguson* was written. We must consider public education in the light of its full development and its present place in American life throughout the Nation." (347 U.S. 492 [1954].) Decisions are reversed as our perception of justice and natural rights develop.

Court decisions around the turn of this century, which declared as unconstitutional a legislative act making it unlawful for an employer to prohibit an employee from joining, or to require him to withdraw from, a trade or labor union or any other lawful organization can hardly serve as precedents in cases in the field of labor law as it exists today, in the wake of the New Deal, the Fair Deal, and the Great Society. Our courts find fewer and fewer occasions to invoke as precedents decisions issued before state welfare became a way of life in the United States. New restraints imposed by labor and civil rights legislation, by the Fair Housing and Equal Employment Opportunity acts, by Affirmative Action and environmental regulation have changed the concepts of "property," "free enterprise," and "liberty" embodied in our laws. The almost unrestrained enjoyment of the use of property and of economic liberty which once characterized our system has disappeared. These changes have both influenced and been influenced by our judicial system.

Court decisions which, after they have been duly tested by experience, are found inconsistent with new conditions or with social welfare are destined for abandonment. Prominent French jurists advocate the judicial interpretation of statutes in *"le sense évolutif"* that calls for inquiring what the legislator would have willed if he had known what the new conditions would be. In the endless process of testing and retesting the structure and desires of our society, precedents must be discarded or modified when they become inconsistent with new rules of conduct and changes in the fundamental desires of the society. As the late Justice William O. Douglas pointed out, the use of precedents or the principle of *stare decisis* "must give way before the dynamic component of history." ("Stare Decisis," *49 Columbia Law Review* 735, 737 [1949].) To paraphrase this statement, we may say that precedents must give way before the compelling force of natural justice and of moral and ethical principles that move forward under the dynamics of human history.

Morals and the Law

The tradition of natural law has a claim on the administration of justice. In my book *The Third Way* (The University of Texas at Dallas, 1980, pp. 155-175), I defended the position that the moral values that underlay the founding of this country can be found in the tradition of natural law. Our basic assertion was and is that the natural law is revealed to mankind for the conservation of man's nature and the promotion of his purpose of existence and well-being. We do not propose to discuss again the merits of this assertion or of the different schools of natural law, but we do wish to dispute the position of those who reject the concept of eternal order by discarding all absolutes, including natural law. The advocates of divorcing the ethical order from the legal admit only the existence of a relationship between morals and the law, not their interdependence. As Holmes expressed it, "The law is the witness and the external deposit of our moral life. The history is the history of the moral development of the race."

There undoubtedly exists "a relationship" between Nazi or Soviet laws and the morality of Hitler, Stalin, and their vicious henchmen. The Nazi and Soviet systems of justice which resulted from such a relationship are fearful examples of the perversion of justice when divorced from the traditional concept of morality. Is it the role of justice to enforce laws which are the "deposit" of a "morality" designed to trample on human lives and rights? No more than other men can judges ignore Edmund Burke's warning, "All that is necessary for the forces of evil to win this world is for good men to do nothing." The courts of

Nazi Germany and of Soviet Russia became agencies subservient to the dictates of the parties in power, carrying out the instructions received from party bosses. The effects are well-known.

The fight against arbitrary tyranny, cynicism, and dictatorship, states Paul Tillich, "can be won only by a new foundation of natural law and justice." *(Love, Power, and Justice,* Oxford University Press, 1954, p. 56.) No one questions the existence of a relationship between "law and the moral development of the race," but it is their interdependence which causes the performance of one's legal duty to include obedience to the urges of morality, revealed to us by the Author of Nature through the force of reason. Such a morality resting on the foundation of a belief in and reverence for the Creator and on obedience to His will enables man to know truth from falsehood, freedom from slavery, and good from evil.

Justice calls for putting into effect the will of the law, but because of the interdependence between moral concern and the exercise of judicial justice, a judge should keep in mind the Psalmist's advice: "Thou hast commanded us to keep thy precepts diligently. O that my ways were directed to keep thy statutes! Then shall I not be ashamed when I have respect unto all thy commandments." (Psalm 119: 4-6.) There no doubt comes a time, wrote Judge Learned Hand, "when a statute is so obviously oppressive and absurd that it can have no justification in any sane polity."

Sir William Blackstone, the English legal commentator who had an immense influence on American jurisprudence, wrote:

"This law of nature being co-eval with mankind and dictated by God himself, is of course superior in obligation to any other. It is binding over all the globe, in all countries, and at all times; no human laws are of any validity, in contrary to this; and such of them as are valid derive all their force, and all their authority mediately or immediately, from the original."

To this powerful statement the famous commentator adds that, in order to apply this law to exigencies that may arise in particular cases, we have to discover "what the law of nature directs in every circumstance of life."

Moral values are more flexible than legal rules in meeting the dictates of natural justice, which responds to the demands of changing "circumstances of life" and new values. Natural justice is universal in its essence and may vary in its applications to particular circumstances. Law is a generative mechanism sharing with Nature the capacity for growth and adaptation. When new conditions arise, old principles may be broadened or adapted to accommodate new insights.

A legislative body is not omnipotent. An act of the legislature contrary to the principles of the Constitution cannot be considered a rightful exercise of legislative authority. It has been repeatedly held that the exercise of police power by a state or municipality gives it authority to enact laws or ordinances which pertain to public safety, public health, or public morals. Since it is a judicial question whether a legislature has transcended the limit of this authority, it is the duty of the courts to look at the substance of legislative action in the field of public safety, health, or morals, subject to constitutional limitations or restraint. In the absence of concrete pronouncements concerning public morals, a judge, as Cardozo expressed it, has to "look into himself," and the moral element enters into his reasoning.

The same free judicial movement takes place when a statute uses representative terms. For instance, in interpreting the constitutional rights of life, liberty, and property—which we shall discuss later—the courts have taken the position that the terms "life," "liberty," and "property" are representative terms and "cover every right to which a member of the body politic is entitled under the law." Their comprehensive scope, according to the courts' interpretation, embraces the rights of self-defense, freedom of speech, religious and political freedom, exemption from arbitrary arrests—"all our liberties, personal, civil, and political—in short, all that makes life worth living." What makes life worth living? The judge must find the answer by looking "into himself" and by searching for the general moral rules which govern society.

As we have mentioned, a number of judges who have written illustrious chapters in the history of our jurisprudence have advocated judicial objectivity as the primary responsibility of the courts. Adhering to the principle *dura lex sed lex* ("Hard law, but the law"), they have advocated the severest intellectual detachment from one's own opinion and the enforcement of laws and contracts in accordance with the evidence and recognized principles of law.

Judges, however, do not live in a vacuum. Review-
ing a case in which the government refused to make
payment to a steel company which had made abnor-
mal profits (22 percent) from the production of ships
during World War I, the Supreme Court took the
position that the government should be held to the
contract unless there were valid and appropriate
reasons known to the law for relieving it from its
obligations. But Justice Frankfurter, who as we have
indicated was one of the most outspoken advocates
of judical objectivity and of "the most alert self-
restraint," wrote in his dissenting opinion: "[T]he
function of the judiciary is not so limited that it must
sanction the use of the federal courts as instruments
of injustice in disregard of moral and equitable principles which have been a part of the law for centuries." (*United States v. Bethlehem Steel Corp.*, 315
U.S. 289, 62 S. Ct. 581 [1942].) Standards of judgment
should not be subjective, but since judges are human
they cannot escape the need to apply standards of
natural justice.

Natural Rights

The concept of natural justice safeguards that of
human rights. In one of the earliest judicial decisions
elaborating on the idea of natural rights, the court
stated, "Due process requires that a person be not
deprived of life, liberty, or property without an opportunity to be heard in defense of his right. *This rule
is founded on principles of natural justice.* [Em-
phasis added.]" (*Stuart v. Palmer*, 74 N.Y. 183, 30
Am. Rep. 289 [1878].) Natural rights are those which

grow out of the nature of man and depend upon his personality. They are distinguished from those which are created by positive laws enacted by a duly constituted government necessary to maintain an orderly organized society.

To discuss the discrepancy assumed by some philosophers between the doctrines of natural law *(lex naturalis)* and natural right *(ius naturae)* over against the individualistic doctrine of natural rights is to prolong an old and often confusing controversy. The meaning of the term "Law of Nature" as used by John Locke is substantially the same as that of "natural right" and "natural rights." Locke greatly influenced Jefferson, and the infusion of the idea of natural rights with the spirit of natural law found its expression in our Declaration of Independence. Locke and Jefferson believed that "man, being the workmanship of one omnipotent and infinitely wise Maker," has rights on his own to freedom, food, shelter, and security—to the satisfaction of fundamental needs. Unless these rights are realized, human life is frustrated, if not impossible.

These natural rights remain constant anytime and anywhere. The Greek Princess Antigone, in Sophocles' drama of the same name, invokes

"The unwritten laws of God that know not change.
They are not of today nor yesterday,
But live forever, nor can man assign
When first they sprang to being."

Thus she defended her disobedience of the tyrant

Creon's decree forbidding her to bury her brother Polyneices' body.

For Cicero the natural law emanates from divine reason "implanted in nature," and natural rights are given by God to man for the promotion of his well-being. According to Grotius and Pufendorf, there is a divinely-originated, universal need for community, and because of man's involvement in the life of society, human rights preserve the community and when enforced sufficiently make life in society tolerable.

According to Locke, men were endowed with certain natural rights before there was a state. Marx, Engels, and Lenin reject his concept of natural law and natural rights. Lenin argued that "law and state are not two distinct phenomena . . . but are two sides of the same phenomenon: class dominance." For Marx a society based on law is a "juridical fiction." Legal relations could not "be explained by the so-called general process of the human mind, but they are rooted in the material conditions of life." Engels wrote that legal principles are "only economic reflexes."

Rejecting the existence of eternal principles, Marx rejected also the existence of natural rights. Since he located the sources of law in the force of production, according to him the material order has priority over the spiritual order. Law, justice, and morality are a superstructure, while economic conditions are the substructure or the foundation of society. Consequently, man is only an economic tool in the hand of the police state. Such neglect of natural human rights brings only tyranny and slavery. The ramifications of such neglect are endless. While our courts, for instance, have stated that "the right of privacy—having its origin in natural law—is immutable and absolute, and transcends the power of any authority to change or abolish it" *(McGovern v. Van Riper,* 137 N.J. Eq. 24, 33, 43 A.2d 514, 519 [1945]), in the omnipotent communist state there is no place for privacy or solitude—unless in a prison cell.

The American conception of natural fundamental rights, which should be beyond the reach of any government, is broader than the protection offered to the English by the Magna Charta, which protects rights only against the monarch. The Magna Charta took the form of prohibitions limiting the power of the King rather than a list of rights such as those embodied in the Constitution of the United States. The Declaration of Independence and Amendments to the Constitution protect these "inalienable rights," based on truths which are "self-evident," against both the executive and legislative branches of government. The independent judiciary, headed by the United States Supreme Court, has the power to declare the acts of the other two branches of government unconstitutional, thus offering an "impenetrable bulwark" against any attempt to violate the natural rights embodied in the Constitution.

Such an "impenetrable bulwark" was envisioned by James Madison when he proposed in the Bill of Rights: "[I]ndependent tribunals of justice will consider themselves in a peculiar manner the guardian of these rights; they will be an impenetrable bulwark against every assumption of power in the legislative or executive." These natural rights include the right to personal liberty, to individual property, to the worship of God according to the dictates of one's own conscience, to equal protection of the laws and to due process of law, to immunity from unreasonable searches and from cruel punishment, and to such other protections as are indispensable to preserve and favor the dignity of man. Because of the most comprehensive scope of human rights, we shall limit our discussion to the so-called trinity of rights, for which—according to our Declaration of Independence—governments among men are instituted: the security of life, liberty, and property guaranteed by the Fifth and Fourteenth Amendments.

The fundamental maxims of a free government require that the established individual rights should be sacred; no government is free to assume the power to violate and disregard them. The first official action of this nation reaffirmed these established principles of private rights by declaring the foundation of government in the following words: "We hold these truths to be self-evident; that all men are created equal, that they are endowed by their Creator with certain inalienable rights; that among these are life, liberty and the pursuit of happiness." These inalienable rights are beyond the control of the state.

The Constitution of the United States should always be read in the thought and spirit of the Declaration of Independence, which was intended to protect persons against the exercise of arbitrary and capricious power by any of the agencies of the federal or state government. A government that avoids interference with these rights held dear by the members of a free society is the only dignified government of men who are conscious of their rights and of the destiny of humanity.

The rights a citizen has to life, liberty, and property are under the protection of the general rules that govern a free society, and no act of legislation can deprive a citizen of these rights. Legislators are sworn to support the Constitution and estopped to deny the existence of the natural rights there asserted. The Constitution grants a restrictive legislative power, within which the legislators must limit their actions for the public welfare, and whose barriers they cannot transcend under the guise of seeking the advance of the welfare of the people. The legislature is not omnipotent, and a law which it may pass to take away life, liberty, or property without a preexisting cause will be an attempt to deprive the citizen of his constitutional rights. The constitutional guaranty nullifies such arbitrary legislation. Legislative judgment or will is not equivalent to the "law of the land."

Trinity of Rights

(1) Liberty and Equality

The Justinian Codification of Roman Law defined justice as "the constant and perpetual disposition to render every man his due." In that comprehensive term "justice" are included the three indispensable rights: the security of life, liberty, and property. These three rights are grouped together and constitute a trinity of rights that are guaranteed against unlawful deprivation by an arbitrary power. Every departure from the safeguards provided by this trinity of rights is apt to be an appropriation of some phase of the totalitarian way.

The full scope of the liberty guaranteed by the Constitution cannot be found in or limited by the precise terms of the specific guarantees provided elsewhere in the Constitution. This liberty, wrote Justice Harlan,

> "is not a series of isolated points pricked out in terms of the taking of property; the freedom of speech, press, and religion; the right to keep and bear arms; the freedom from unreasonable searches and seizures; and so on. It is a rational continuum which, broadly speaking, includes a freedom from all substantial arbitrary impositions and purposeless restraints ... and which also recognizes, what a reasonable and sensitive judgment must, that certain interests require particularly careful scrutiny of the state needs asserted to justify their abridgment." (*Poe v. Ullman,* 367 U.S. 497, 543, 81 S. Ct. 1752, 1776, 6 L. Ed. 2d 989 [1961].)

The term "liberty" is deemed to embrace the right of man to be free in the enjoyment of the faculties with which he has been endowed by his Creator, subject only to such restraints as are necessary for the common welfare. "Liberty," as used in the federal and state constitutions, in a negative sense means freedom from restraint; in a positive sense, it means the freedom obtained by the imposition of restraint needed to promote the greatest possible amount of liberty for each. In other words, "liberty" is freedom from all restraints except such as are justly imposed by law. The interest of society calls for the absence of arbitrary restraint and not for immunity from reasonable regulations.

By the imposition upon particular persons of restraints which are deemed necessary for the general welfare, individuals give up some natural rights in consideration of equal protection and opportunity. The Bill of Rights does not license any individual to defy or ignore the correlative rights of other individuals or of society. So far as it is noticed by government, explained the court, liberty is restraint rather than license. "It is yielding of the individual will to that of many, subject to such constitutional guarantees or limitations as will preserve those rights and privileges which are admitted of all men to be fundamental." *(Weber v. Doust,* 84 Wash. 330, 146 P. 623, 625 [1915].)

Every citizen is allowed so much liberty as may exist without impairment of the *equal* rights of his fellows. Equality is an attribute of liberty. The Fourteenth Amendment intended not only that there should be no arbitrary deprivation of life, liberty, or property, but also that equal protection and security should be given to all under like circumstances in the enjoyment of their personal and civil rights. We stress the reference to "like circumstances." The "equal protection" clause of the Fourteenth Amendment means that equality is obtained if the citizen's civil rights are secured to him in the same manner and to the same extent as the same rights are accorded to all other persons under "similar circumstances."

Equality is not unlimited and cannot be maximized at the expense of liberty. It should be remembered that men are not born with equal powers and faculties; they should be offered all opportunities to develop their talents, and their creative abilities should have full opportunity of expression. Egalitarianism, which calls for the achievement of equality of conditions, leads to mediocrity and the deprivation of the citizen of his individual liberty, especially of his freedom of enterprise exercised under the principle of equality of opportunity.

All citizens are born to equal opportunities, equal political and civil rights. All citizens have equal access to the courts for the equal protection of their persons and liberties. The equal protection of laws is a pledge of the protection of equal laws. When the Assembly of the Province of Pennsylvania in 1751 ordered a bell to commemorate the fifteeth anniversary of William Penn's Charter of Privileges, which ensured freedom for all citizens of the province, it decided to inscribe on the bell's shoulder the biblical phrase: "Proclaim liberty throughout *all* the land unto *all* the inhabitants thereof." (Leviticus 25:10.)

(2) Right to Life and Privacy

The term "life" as employed in the Fifth and Fourteenth Amendments is a representative term. It means something more than mere animal existence. Life is a right inherent by nature in every individual which prohibits not only the mutilation of the body or destruction of any of its organs, but also prohibits the deprivation of whatever God has given to everyone with life for its enjoyment and growth. As a member of organized society, the individual surrenders to society many rights and privileges which he would be free to exercise in a state of nature, but he is not presumed to surrender rights recognized as personal, absolute, and inalienable. Among these rights is that of personal privacy.

The right of privacy, as our courts have explained, has its foundations in the instincts of nature. "It is recognized intuitively, consciousness being the witness to prove its existence." *(Bednarik v. Bednarik,* 16 A.2d 80, 18 N.J. Misc. 6331 [1940].) Derived from natural law, the concept of the right of privacy was developed under the Roman law and became incorporated into our common law. The person's right "to be let alone" is the foundation of the common law maxim, which is more than an epigram, that "every man's house is his castle," and of the law concerning unreasonable searches and seizures. The right of every person to be free from the scrutiny of others with respect to his private affairs was invoked in the most sensitive and emotional issue of abortion.

The Supreme Court in its opinion, delivered in 1973, held that the constitutional right of privacy encompasses woman's decision whether or not to terminate her pregnancy in the first trimester of pregnancy, so long as she can find a physician willing to administer an abortion. *(Roe v. Wade,* 410 U.S. 113 [1973].) The right to terminate pregnancy is, therefore, not absolute and is subject to limitations. The State does have an important, constitutionally justifiable interest in preserving and protecting the health of the pregnant woman as well as the potentiality of human life.

With respect to the health of the mother, the Court concluded that the "compelling" point is at approximately the end of the first trimester. The conclusion is based on the fact that until the end of the first trimester mortality in abortion may be less than mortality in normal childbirth. The State retains a definite interest in protecting the mother's health when an abortion is considered at a later stage of pregnancy. Therefore, after the first trimester the State may, if it chooses, regulate the abortion procedure. As to the fetus, the "compelling" point is at viability, that is, when the fetus is potentially able to live outside the mother's womb, although aided by artificial means.

The *Roe v. Wade* decision inspired a raging dispute. It became an issue in the 1980 presidential campaign and continues to be a subject of a heated controversy in the Congress. Deep convictions are behind the vigorous opposing views. One point of view asserts that one has an unlimited right to do with one's body as one pleases. Those who challenge state abortion laws point out that, when most abortion laws were first enacted, the abortion procedure was a hazardous one and that the State's interest focussed on protecting the woman's health rather than in preserving the embryo and fetus. Because medical advances have lessened this concern, at least with respect to abortion in early pregnancy, such abortion laws can thus no longer be justified by any State interest.

The other point of view argues that life begins at conception and is present throughout pregnancy, and that therefore the State has a compelling interest in protecting life from and after conception. This interest goes beyond the protection of the pregnant woman alone; the State's interest and general obligation extends to prenatal life. Since human life, as protected under the Constitution, begins with the conception, abortion would be murder.

In reaching the *Roe v. Wade* decision, the Supreme Court did not find the need to resolve the difficult question of when life begins. "When those," wrote the Court, "trained in the respective disciplines of medicine, philosophy, and theology are unable to arrive at any consensus, the judiciary, at this point in the development of man's knowledge, is not in a position to speculate as to the answer."

It is difficult "to speculate as to the answer" when attitudes toward the discussed question represent a wide divergence of not always consistent thinking. For instance, the present official belief of the Catholic Church calls for recognition of the existence of life from the moment of conception. In 1869 Pope Pius IX decreed that the soul enters the egg at conception. Yet until the nineteenth century the Aristotelian theory of "mediate animation" served as the official Roman Catholic dogma. The fetus became "animated" when it was infused with a soul. Christian theology and canon law determined the point of animation of forty days for a male and eighty days for a female. Accordingly, St. Augustine made a distinction between *embryo inanimatus* ("not yet endowed with a soul") and *embryo animatus*.

Thomas Aquinas defined movement as one of the first principles of life. The thirteenth-century English judge and writer Henry de Bracton (like most of the lawyers of his time, a priest) focussed on the quickening of the fetus as the critical point, and abortion of the quickened fetus was, in his opinion, homicide. Blackstone believed that life is the immediate gift of God and begins, in contemplation of law, as soon as an infant is able to stir in the mother's womb.

One's personal experiences, religious training, attitudes toward the family, and established moral standards will influence his conclusions whether to follow the opinion that the embryo is just a portion of the mother—not a moral or personal being—or to accept the belief so explicitly expressed by the German theologian Dietrich Bonhoeffer that "God certainly intended to create a human being" in the fetus and that by abortion "this nascent human being has been deliberately deprived of his life and that is nothing but murder."

The abortion controversy will remain highly sensitive and emotional. A statement free of emotion and of predilection can be made that the vigorous dispute on this matter demonstrates the importance of the natural right to life. It exists inherently in every man by endowment of the Creator. This right, which appertains originally and essentially to man, was wisely reaffirmed in the Constitution.

(3) Right to Property: Police Power and Eminent Domain

The third absolute right inherent in every man is the right to property, which provides all persons with equal protection and security in the free acquisition, use, enjoyment, and disposal of property. David Hume (1711-1776), the Scottish historian and philosopher whose *Treatise of Human Nature* greatly influenced our federal and state constitutions, considered that the peace and security of human society depend upon three fundamental laws: stability of possession, its transference by consent, and the performance of promises.

On a similar note the prominent American jurist, James Kent (1763-1847), who served as Chancellor of the Court of Chancery in New York and upon his retirement from the court as a professor at Columbia University, stressed the importance of the right to property when he wrote:

> "The sense of property is graciously bestowed on mankind for the purpose of rousing them from sloth and stimulating them to action, and as long as the right of acquisition is exercised in conformity to the social relations, and the moral obligations which spring from them, it ought to be sacredly protected. The natural and active sense of property pervades the foundation of social improvement. It leads to the cultivation of the earth, the institution of government, the establishment of justice, the acquisition of the comforts of life, the growth of the useful arts, the spirit of commerce, the productions of taste, the erections of charity, and the display of the benevolent affections."

Kent believed that "human society would be in a most unnatural and miserable condition" if it would follow the speculations of the modern theorists who consider inequalities in property and the right to "separate and exclusive" property as the cause of injustice, and of the "unhappy result of government and artificial institutions."

The term "property," like the terms "life" and

"liberty," is also a representative term. It carries
with it as its natural and necessary coincident all that
effectuates and renders complete the full, unrestrained enjoyment of that right. Within its comprehensive scope are embraced—as our courts have
explained—every auxiliary right, every attribute
necessary to make the principal right to property
effectual and valuable in its most extensive sense.
No person shall be deprived of his property rights by
an arbitrary power in any form. Where rights of property are admitted to exist, neither the legislative,
executive, nor judicial agencies can declare they
shall exist no longer. Prohibition, regulation, or interference with the right to property can be upheld
only under the police power rightfully exercised for
the protection of the public safety, the public health,
or the public morals.

Blackstone defines the term "police" as "the due
regulation and domestic order of the kingdom,
whereby the individuals of the state, like members of
a well governed family, are bound to conform their
general behavior to the rules of propriety, good
neighborhood, and good manners, and to be decent,
industrious, and inoffensive in their respective sta-
tions." The state's or municipality's authority to
enact legislation for the protection of the public
safety, the public health, or the public morals grows
out of what is known as its "police power." This
power is inherent in every sovereignty to govern
men and things under which the legislature may
within constitutional limitation prescribe regulations to promote the public health, morals, and safety
and add to the general public prosperity and welfare.

Of course, the regulations cannot be unreasonably arbitrary or capricious.

Police power regulates the use of property or impairs rights in property when free exercise of these rights is detrimental to public interest. Appropriation of property takes place for the purpose of destruction when it is dangerous or by the way of confiscation as a penalty. When the property is dangerous, it is not taken for public use but for destruction in order to promote general welfare. Protection of life is of greater importance than the protection of private property rights. The owner is not compensated for any damage he may sustain since he is sufficiently compensated by sharing in the general benefits resulting from the exercise of the police power.

Police power and eminent domain have been sometimes confused. Eminent domain power is the right of the government acting in the interest of the public to force the owner of the property to sell the same to the public. The constitutions adopted by the states and the Fourteenth Amendment guarantee the owner fair and adequate compensation and due process. Eminent domain takes property because it is useful to the public. The "public purpose" is viewed in the light of technical development and economic and social conditions. When public need requires the acquisition of private property, eminent domain power protects the public from being deprived of the needed public service if the owner refuses to sell his property or from paying an excessive price demanded by an owner.

The state or municipality takes property under the

eminent domain power because it is useful to the public, and under police power because it is harmful or it is the cause of the public detriment. The destruction of property to avert impending peril, as to prevent the spread of fire, is an exercise of the police power. Taking of property for the building of roads, streets, highways, water reservoirs, hospitals, and schools and for many other services meeting the needs of the public is an exercise of the eminent domain power. Police power when exercised within its legitimate limits requires no compensation, whereas eminent domain recognizes a right to compensation. Both powers enable government to carry out the purposes for which they were organized under the respective federal and state constitutions.

Both powers are founded in public necessity, and only public necessity can justify their exercise. Arbitrary legislation which passes under the guise of the police power is void. Also void is any legislation if it serves no useful purpose to advance public welfare or if the restriction of private rights is oppressive and the public welfare is enhanced only in slight degree. The Constitution permits no excessive encroachment upon the private right of property. Only the attainment of some public object of sufficient necessity and importance can justify the exertion of these powers. Private rights to property should never be sacrificed to a greater extent than necessary. The fundamental maxims of a free government do not leave the rights of property solely dependent upon the will of the legislative body, nor would any court of justice in this country be warranted in assuming an arbitrary power to violate and disregard the right to property, which should be held sacred.

Political Significance of the Trinity of Rights

As mentioned earlier, these are rights in every society which are beyond the control of the government. When on April 25, 1775, the people of Philadelphia received the news of the Battle of Lexington, the bell called together over 8000 patriots who assembled in the Statehouse yard and agreed unanimously "to associate for the purpose of defending with arms, our lives, liberty, and property against all attempts to deprive us of them."

The trinity of rights encompasses a broad group of rights recognized in a free society to which we have referred before, namely the right to be free from governmental violations of the integrity of the person—violations such as torture; cruel, inhuman, or degrading punishment; invasion of the home; arbitrary arrest or imprisonment; and denial of public trial. Among the numerous reflections of the right to liberty, we may list the right to follow one's conscience; the right to enter into contracts and to acquire and to enjoy property; the right to travel freely within and outside one's own country; the right to be free from discrimination based on race, religion, or sex; and the right to enjoy civil and political rights, including freedom of speech, press, religion, and assembly.

We have referred to rights in a "free society," not in a "democracy"—although in the past the terms have been used almost interchangeably—because on the contemporary international stage we find many governments fraudulently using the terminology of democracy or of "people's democracy." The totalitarian regimes fraudulently refer to the people as a source of their legitimacy, and their constitutions, elections, and representative assemblies are meaningless. The dictator and the political party in power reject in principle the idea of human rights and rule through a massive bureaucratic and police apparatus. Efforts to create freer and more pluralistic societies are met with tanks, imprisonment, torture, and exile.

The rights to liberty, life, and property are "inalienable." The Declaration of Independence states, "To secure these rights, governments are instituted among men, deriving their just powers from the consent of the governed." The rights of the individual are not derived from governmental agencies, or even from the Constitution. They exist by the endowment of the Creator, and are merely reaffirmed in the Constitution. The government's authority comes from the people. In other words, we are self-governing people, and our government was not designed to be paternal in form.

Our entire social and political structure rests upon the cornerstone that all men have certain rights that are inherent. These natural rights may not be transgressed with impunity nor disregarded because of expedience; neither may they be abrogated, abridged, or suspended by any human enactment because they are based on "the laws of nature and of nature's God," on truths which are "self-evident." The self-evident truth, we repeat, is that "all men are created equal, that they are endowed by their Creator with certain inalienable rights."

JUDGMENT, JUSTICE, AND MERCY

by

Barry Bailey

Barry Bailey

Dr. Bailey has been Senior Minister of the First United Methodist Church in Fort Worth, Texas, since 1976. He preaches live over television every Sunday morning via KTVT-TV and is seen in nine states by means of Community Antenna Systems.

Dr. Bailey received his undergraduate education at Hendrix College in Conway, Arkansas, and earned his Master of Theology degree from Perkins School of Theology at Southern Methodist University in Dallas, Texas, and his Doctor of Divinity degree from Centenary College in Shreveport, Louisiana. He was awarded a Doctor of Letters degree by Southwestern University in Georgetown, Texas.

An ordained Methodist minister and a member of the Central Texas Annual Conference, Dr. Bailey has been guest preacher for many conferences and church and community events. He has also addressed many ministers conferences and taken part in many lecture series throughout the Southwest.

Beyond his local church responsibilities, Dr. Bailey is president-elect of the Tarrant Area Community of Churches and was a delegate to the General Conference of the United Methodist Church. He is a Trustee of Southern Methodist University, Texas Wesleyan College, and Harris Hospital-Methodist of Fort Worth.

Dr. Bailey is the author of four books: Especially for You *(1978);* We Are Not Alone *(1979);* Living With Your Feelings *(1980); and* With Best Wishes *(1982).*

JUDGMENT, JUSTICE, AND MERCY

by

Barry Bailey

A scripture in the Old Testament is probably one of the greatest theological statements made anywhere, from any religion: "What does the Lord require of you, but to do justice, to love mercy, and to walk humbly with your God?" It seems to me that for us today, as we live in this world with billions of people and with various kinds of possibilities for destroying each other, that question is not only theological, but very practical and pragmatic as well.

By and large, I think theology emerges out of psychology. Regardless of what lofty ideas we may have about the presence of God, when we are frightened, we may pray as a little child, saying, "O God, get me through the night." At times, every one of us has a need for something we can touch, something we can handle, something with which we can identify; but when anyone feels so insecure that he continuously clings to his religion like a security blanket, his judgment may be impaired. On the other hand, the main thrust of theology should not be toward making us more liberal, but toward encouraging us to become more open. No one could be more narrow than a liberal who is determined that we must agree with him or her.

Too often, we let fear, superstition, or tradition take control of our lives, and we may never look back and reexamine the creed we profess to live by. If I argue with you and win the argument, I may view that as proof that I am right. Suppose you are right, but I still win the argument; what effect will that have on each of us? You could have helped me grow, but I won the argument when I was wrong. I believe that in education, in religion, and in life, we must have a commonsense approach to the things that are dear to us. If you have an idea that is vital to you, that you believe is essential, you should examine it, question it, and give yourself a chance to grow. Otherwise, we make icons out of our own beliefs. I think that the more zealous your religious devotion is, the more dangerous it becomes unless you approach it with discernment. When you look at history, you find that some of the most atrocious wars ever fought were fought under the guise of "religious wars"; but there never was a "holy" war. Therefore, we ought to question the beliefs to which we cling so tenaciously.

To me, the three ingredients—judgment, justice, and mercy—compose almost a tripod to support a society or a religion, and they are so intertwined that it is difficult to separate them. I would suggest that justice is negated, and so is mercy, unless we have the ability to judge the situations we face with discernment. That ability is often in short supply, and what masquerades, sometimes, as enlightened judgment actually is prejudice. Unless we use common sense in the judgments we make, religious devotion, as well as patriotism, can become fanatical.

Patriotic zeal must be tempered with judgment. If we flip our minds back a few years in our nation's history, we will remember Senator Joseph McCarthy, who vowed to point out the enemy of America, to point out the Communists, and to point out other groups he labeled "subversive"—he assured us he could identify them. Do you know what happened? Many believed him! And fear permeated our land. Many people lost their jobs or were blacklisted just because McCarthy said they were communistic. At one time, even the Girl Scouts were on his list, and the people of America were so caught up in fear that they did not even recognize the humor in that accusation. When a nation loses its sense of humor, it has a problem, indeed. There we were, afraid of each other, until one day someone began to question the Senator, and things began to change drastically. Why did we wait so long? If we are to have justice, if we are to have mercy, if we are going to have a healthy society, you and I must have enlightened judgment.

In the church, we often find ourselves applauding the person who knows all the answers and professes his or her great faith without any hesitation whatsoever. Too often, we are witnessing a lot of heat, but very little light. In the church, we encourage great faith and we reward it, because we feel threatened by doubters. I suspect that your faith and your belief have very little substance if you have not examined every premise that is presented to you very carefully. That is called questing; it brings about growth. In this sense, Jesus' statement "Come and follow me" is an invitation to grow. Consequently, what I desire for my own life, what I desire for the church, and what I desire for America is that we open our minds and use our good common sense as we consider any situation.

In the Old Testament, we read of the time when Abraham was about to offer his son Isaac to show his dedication to God. That was what he understood was required of him. He took the young boy to the place where he intended to make his sacrifice, and when he was about to kill his own son, he realized there was a ram in the bushes nearby. He stopped, took the ram, and offered it to God. And Isaac was saved.

Many people see that story as an indication of Abraham's great devotion to God. They say, "He was being tested, and he would have killed Isaac to prove his love for God." That is one interpretation, but is it not possible that Abraham's understanding of God was meager and limited then, as ours is now, and that he misunderstood what God expected of him? Here was a man, frantically asking himself, "What am I going to do?" He was about to make the wrong decision, however you explain it. A ram was there, and he offered the ram. Was it necessary that an animal be sacrificed? That was what he believed out of his culture. What do we think in America today? When you come right down to it, when we think about religion, do not many of us think that somebody has to pay the price? That is what we say about Jesus—"No more rams, no more bullocks, no more pigeons, no more doves—Jesus hung on the cross and paid it all, and now God will take us back." What kind of God do you have that works that way?

Your judgment must be enlightened if justice is to prevail. It is vital that we get our facts straight. Years ago, when I was a freshman in college, I was called into the Dean's office one day. I went, thinking he wanted to discuss some work we had done. When I sat down, be began to question me, and I realized that I was being accused of something, but I had no idea what it could be. After a lengthy discussion, he finally said that I had stolen something. Now, I may have done other things, but I did not remember ever stealing anything in my life, and I told him so.

Our conversation continued for nearly an hour before he said, at last, "Well, you have some marked money in your pocket." I could not believe it. He told me that somebody had been stealing money from the canteen, and I had fallen into a trap that was set to catch the thief. I told him that when I was in the canteen earlier, another student had a number of 50-cent pieces and said he did not want to carry all that change, so I exchanged some of my bills for the change he had. The Dean questioned the young man I had named, who admitted that he had been taking the money for a long time. I had the marked money and I was considered guilty, but I was innocent. That experience taught me that when we know we are right, we may be mistaken. We should withhold judgment until we have examined it very carefully because, so often, things are not as they appear. What began as judgment against me emerged as justice when it was enlightened by the truth.

How long did America live with segregation? Often we accepted, without question, the lies we were told about black people—that they liked hard, heavy work; that they did not need as much money as we had to take care of their families; that they kind of liked living in little quarters to themselves, because they wanted to be together. They were different. We gave tacit approval to segregation by failing to speak out against it. It is almost inconceivable to me now that we failed to see the inconsistency between our attitude toward segregation and the Christian gospel we claimed to embrace. As long as we allowed ourselves to believe the lies we had been told, we could call Jesus Christ our "Lord and Saviour" without feeling guilty about the discrimination we practiced. We believed that if we walked down the aisle of the church and came to God, he would save our souls without calling us to account for the injustice we were perpetrating on the black people.

Once, a young black man walked into a white cafe in a Southern town, sat down at the lunch counter, and ordered some food. He refused to move, even when he was told, "If you sit there any longer you will be arrested." So he was arrested and taken to jail. He had no thought of leading a movement against segregation. Often you find that the person who is the leader did not choose that role. Even Moses tried to avoid becoming a leader until that role was thrust upon him.

What was this young man doing? I will tell you what he was doing. He was saving our people, as well as his. Slavery was hard on everyone, the slave owner and the slave, for if I am allowed to mistreat you, in the long run my actions probably will diminish me more than they diminish you. But when our judgment is enlightened, we begin to seek justice, and mercy follows as a natural by-product.

Judgment must be discerning. If you are my friend, you may judge me; but after you have done so, you will help me. Suppose you are trying to help me understand some subject you know well, such as mathematics; first you determine how much I already know about it, then you will be able to open new doors of learning for me, because you care.

Certainly, God's judgment has about it a quality of caring. Sometime ago I read a delightful collection of stories of the Midrash—the Jewish teachings which are used with the Torah, particularly in teaching young people. The book I read was a collection of stories and teachings, with questions and answers. It is not a catechism, but it develops underlying thoughts that are not apparent on the surface. It has been collected from rabbis for centuries.

I was especially interested in one particular story which included the question, "When the Israelite people were brought out of Egypt and had gone through the Red Sea and were safe on the other side, and the Egyptian army followed them and was drowned in the Red Sea, what did God do?" In many Christian Sunday School classes, I imagine the response might be, "What do you mean, 'What did God do?'—God had his way; He did it; He killed the Egyptians, because they were mistreating the Jews." A Christian might typically respond like that, without ever raising the question, "What kind of God would you have who would do that?" We know that one of the Commandments says, "Thou shall not kill." Can God break his own law and still maintain his own integrity? I love the answer to the question "What did God do?" in the Midrash I read; it is laconic, and very much to the point: "God wept, because God loved the Egyptians, too." That comes from Jewish teachings, and it shows a perception of God that Christians would do well to emulate. It is

important that we develop such an awareness that
goes beyond our own culture, our own security, our
own protection, so that we honestly try to grow in our
relationships with other people and learn to show
them mercy.

For a long time I thought that most of us sought
justice, but I no longer believe that, because I have
found that justice presents problems for us. Sometimes we demand justice so long as it benefits us, but
if justice means that someone else will reap the rewards, we are not so sure that is how we want it. In
the story of the Prodigal Son, the young man comes
back home and is welcomed by his father with open
arms. The elder brother's judgment is obscured by
what he perceives as injustice to himself. He becomes angry and refuses to go into the house. He fails
to show mercy to his brother.

On the other hand, Jesus' judgment was clear
when he walked into the temple and turned over the
tables of the moneychangers. Jesus was interested in
seeing that justice was done, and he showed mercy
toward those people he saw being manipulated. It is
so difficult to be just that, unless we are discerning in
our judgment, most of us will try to bypass justice
altogether. It takes more courage than many of us can
muster.

Quite some time ago I read about what some historians consider one of the most significant events in
our history. Andrew Johnson succeeded to the presidency upon the death of Abraham Lincoln, and he
began trying to carry out Lincoln's proposal to get the
South back into the Union to heal the wound the
Civil War had left. However, some people wanted to

punish the South for seceding and began a drive for Johnson's impeachment. At that time, thirty-six votes were required in the Senate to convict him. When the leaders took a count, they thought they had enough votes. But one man did not vote the way he was expected to, and the result was thirty-five votes for conviction—one short.

It was common knowledge that Edmund G. Ross, a Senator from Kansas, did not like the President. For this reason, he was expected to turn the tide for conviction. He had received letters, insults, and threats. He had even been offered $40,000 to vote for conviction. But, at the time of the vote, when his name was called, he stood up and said, "Not guilty!" The roll had to be called all the way through, but as soon as Ross cast his vote, it was clear that the effort to convict Johnson had failed. The Senator was quoted as saying, when he voted as he did. "I looked down into my own grave." I suppose, in a political sense, he did. He was accused of being disloyal to his country and was rejected, humiliated, and ostracized. From our vantage point, more than 100 years later, it is easy for us to think that Ross did the right thing, "just what we would have done," but I believe that one of the hardest things for anyone to do is to be fair. Justice often calls itself "fairness" when, in reality, it is "prejudice" unless it is viewed from the proper perspective.

What does God require of us in our religion? Or what is required of America in relation to the world? You and I love our country, and people all over the world love theirs, I am sure. The problem today is that hardly anybody loves our world, so we go from one war to another. It is good that we love our country, but someone must take a larger view and care about humanity. We should be enlightened enough to realize that it is possible to demonstrate our love for America in other ways besides fighting for our country. If that is not true, the great religious teachers of the world have been wrong; and the great political science scholars of the world, too, have been wrong, because this has been a common theme in their teachings. We need to deal fairly and openly with people. Once we begin to do that, it is amazing how our understanding of them and their needs can grow.

As I speak of dealing with other nations of the world, I am aware that today is Veterans' Day, November 11. Early this morning, when I went out to get the newspaper, I saw a picture that stabbed me awake. It showed a young man whose right leg had been amputated, leaning on a crutch as he looked at the newly constructed monument to the Vietnam War veterans. I have no idea what he was thinking as he stood there, but I know what I was thinking as I looked at it. It is easy for someone like me to criticize our involvement in the Vietnam War, which I despised at the time. But in my criticism of the Vietnam War, should I condemn an individual who went because he was drafted, however foolish and insane the war might have been?

This young man went to war, and I am not the person I should be if I can look at his picture without considering that he has gone through hell. He paid an enormous price personally, and no doubt he did things that embarrassed him. He must have memories he would give almost anything to erase. Would it not be callous of me to stand here and criticize what took place several years ago and feel no compassion toward those who were a part of it?

We should achieve enlightened judgment which pushes us out into the realm of justice, where we want to be fair. As we try to be fair, however, we know that somebody will be hurt. If we work at it long enough, we may start caring about people, and when we care about people, mercy prevails. Mercy is the quality that allows me to see in you something that I see within myself. I am sure that there are areas of your life where you can be embarrassed and where you feel awkward. There are other areas where you are strong and productive. As I look at you closely, suddenly I begin to see that there are things in your life that dissatisfy you, just as there are things in my life that I would like to change. We discover that we are very much alike. And now, if I can begin to appreciate myself, it may follow that I will begin to appreciate you, too.

Probably the Civil War provided us with as much romantic literature as any period in our history. Certainly we are familiar with *Gone With The Wind*, and there have been many other stories. Recently I read a marvelous biography of Robert E. Lee by Charles B. Flood entitled *Lee: The Lost Years* (Houghton Mifflin, 1981). In it I encountered a story that was completely new to me. I checked it out and learned that it was factual, as far as I could determine. Of course, I had read about the Appomattox surrender, as you have. But this story presented some interesting insights that I did not remember.

The surrender took place on Palm Sunday 1865 at Appomattox, Virginia. For weeks, Lee had realized that surrender was inevitable; it was only a question of when. He decided he would send word to General Grant that he was ready to surrender to him. Once he wrote the letter, it took two hours for the word to reach General Grant; then, of course, word spread as quickly as the men could pass it around, and the fighting stopped.

The two men were to meet at Appomattox, and General Lee arrived first. General Grant came later, because he was farther away. As they began to talk, General Grant tried to ease the tenseness of the situation as much as possible, because he had great respect for Lee. He talked about the Mexican War and told different stories, and it seemed as if they would never get around to discussing the purpose of their meeting. After about an hour, General Lee said to General Grant, "Sir, you know why we are here," and Grant replied "Yes." Finally, they began to discuss the surrender.

General Lee asked, "What will you require of me?" Grant answered, "The same things that I sent you word about earlier." Lee was afraid that Grant would be harder on him, now that he was actually going to surrender. But Grant said, "I have told you that your men will not be tried, and they will not be prisoners of war; they can all go back home. I told you that your officers can keep their horses and guns." So Lee thanked him and said, "I know you have said that my officers can keep their guns and horses, but what about my men? It is nearly planting time, and they can't make it without their horses."

And General Grant said, "I won't change what I have written here, but I will send word that they may keep their horses." After thanking him, Lee said, "Sir, we have 1,000 or 1,500 prisoners—your men—whom we have captured, and they have not eaten for quite awhile, because we had no rations to give them." General Grant agreed to take them immediately and begin to take care of them.

When that was settled, Grant sensed that Lee had yet another concern, and he asked, "General, would you like some rations for your men?" General Lee replied, "Yes, sir, I would." But he did not know how many soldiers he had, because they were scattered. Now, think of this: A war has just ended—a Civil War that split our country wide open, with friend killing friend and relative killing relative—and Grant, this giant of a man, asks Lee, "Would 25,000 rations do?" Lee replied, "That's plenty." Do you realize that a victorious army was giving food to an army they had defeated? That happened in our country, but I did not know the story until I read that book recently.

War is hell. Mercy comes, not when you do what you are required to do, what you are coerced to do, but when, out of strength, you voluntarily do something just because it is the right thing to do. That is not weakness; it is the hope of the world. However, I think that mercy will sometimes masquerade as sentimentality, calling itself love. Unless we get our facts straight, unless we are discerning, we will not know how to be merciful.

One final thing I want to say concerns the way we learn the truth. Look at the people who make your life better, people to whom you are indebted, people

you treasure. They may never be aware that they
have helped you at all. Think of the people you may
have helped without realizing it. It is not necessary
that we brag on each other, but we do grow with each
other just by being together, by being there for each
other.

Toward the end of the musical *Camelot*, Arthur
has lost Guinevere; he has lost the Round Table; he
has lost his reign, really his throne; and to a great
degree, he has lost his friend, Lancelot. In one of the
last scenes, he is shown with a young boy, Tom.
Arthur is thinking aloud. As he talks about wanting
the boy to remember Camelot, he says,

> "Yes, Camelot—
> Where once it never rained 'til after sundown;
> By eight a.m. the morning fog had flown;
> Let it never be forgot that once there was a spot,
> For one brief, shining moment, that was known
>   as Camelot."

He turns to young Tom and tells him to kneel and
then he takes his sword, Excalibur, and says, "I dub
thee Sir Tom of Warwick." The boy asks what he is
supposed to do and is told, "Run, run and tell the
story." At the end you hear Arthur's voice saying,
"Run, Tom, run."

This is our country, and you and I love it although
we never really know what makes a country great. I
suppose it is the vast realm of ideas that makes a
difference. D votion alone can become dangerous,
unless it is tempered with judgment. Ideas, unless
they catch fire, unless they are harnessed to something, can become utterly useless. However, when

we use common sense in our judgments and work diligently for justice, a passion for the quality of mercy in our lives may result. Perhaps, if we listen, we may hear someone saying to us, "Run and tell the story."

What does the Lord require of us? Is it not "to be just, love mercy, and walk humbly with God?"

JUSTICE AND SOCIETY: BEYOND INDIVIDUALISM

by

Ewell E. Murphy, Jr.

Ewell E. Murphy, Jr.

Mr. Murphy is a Senior Partner and head of the International Department of Baker & Botts, Houston's oldest law firm.

A native of Washington, D.C., Mr. Murphy was educated in the public schools and junior college of San Angelo, Texas, and at the University of Texas , where he received his B.A. and LL.B. degrees with honors. As a Rhodes Scholar he subsequently studied comparative law at Oxford University, England, where he was awarded the degree of Doctor of Philosophy in 1951.

During the Korean War he served in the U.S. Air Force, principally in Dhahran as a judge advocate officer with the United States Mission to Saudi Arabia.

Mr. Murphy has been associated with Baker & Botts since 1954, becoming a Partner in 1964 and a Senior Partner in 1980. He has served as Chairman of the International Law Section of the American Bar Association and a member of the governing councils of The American Society of International Law and the Inter-American Bar Association. He is a trustee of The Southwestern Legal Foundation and a member of the Advisory Board of the Foundation's International and Comparative Law Center. His civic activities have included the presidency of both the Houston World Trade Association and the Houston Philosophical Society and the chairmanship of the International Business Committee of the Houston Chamber of Commerce.

A frequent lecturer on legal topics, Mr. Murphy has published more than twenty articles on subjects of international business law and legal philosophy. In 1980 he received the Carl H. Fulda Award of the Texas International Law Journal for outstanding achievement in the field of international law.

JUSTICE AND SOCIETY: BEYOND INDIVIDUALISM

by

Ewell E. Murphy, Jr.

A Mortician's Smile

They were such very different men: George Orwell the introspective observer, self-made proletarian, Marxist turned anti-Communist, crafter of the cleanest English prose of his generation; André Malraux the flamboyant adventurer, soldier of fortune and conviction, eloquent philosopher of art, Minister of Culture to the most culture-conscious nation on earth. How remarkable it is, that they should have come their very different paths to a common intuition of the most significant transformation of our century. "We live in an age," Orwell observed in 1941, "in which the autonomous individual is ceasing to exist—or perhaps one ought to say, in which the individual is ceasing to have the illusion of being autonomous." "Individualism," Malraux agreed thirty-five years later, "was blown to pieces by the atomic bomb . . ."

What was this individualism, whose demise (or the demise of whose myth) these wise men sensed? Its focus was the single human being. It viewed him—not his family, his community, his clan, his nation, or his race, but singly him—as the unit structure of society. Of that extrapolated monad, the individual, it said three things. First, that reality was what he separately perceived. Second, that the good was what he perceived to be separately beneficial to his separate self. Third, that the justness of a society was measured by the number of immunities it afforded him, the individual, against the group.

If individualism is dead, as Orwell and Malraux believed, it nonetheless beguiles us from its coffin with a persuasive mortician's smile of pseudo-immortality. Only by reentering history and reenacting the metamorphosis of man's self-image can we experience the yet more persuasive truth that individualism, like every other human institution, was mortal; that man did not—and will not—always regard himself that way. I ask that for a short while you suspend disbelief, depart the twentieth century, erase each preconception of yourself, and join me in that arduous reenacting. It will be a tragedy in five acts, the psychodrama of Western man. The protagonist is you.

An Arduous Reenacting

Act I: The time is 12,000 B.C.; the place, a cave above the Dordogne River. It is a winter night. A score of fur-clad figures encircle a smoky fire. Two women turn reindeer haunches over glowing coals. Several men are scraping hides with sharp flint-bladed hafts. A white-bearded elder wearing a long necklace of animal teeth reverently brushes ochre within a bison's silhouette on the limestone wall. In an alcove a heap of skins convulses with the keening moans of a young woman in labor, her face contorted and perspiring, the small stone figure of a naked, erotically obese female locked in her frightened fist.

You are one of the wide-eyed children who squat before the fire. You observe it all—the preparing of food, the working of pelts, the invocation of deities of hunt and birth—but you do not observe that you observe. It is as though your perception, like every other activity of the group, were communal—that the stench of searing flesh strikes a common nostril, a single hand works the hides and tints the bison-god, all writhe in childbirth. In this your group about the fire there is no individual. The unit is the clan.

Act II: Athens, an evening in early summer, 415 B.C. You are a flute-girl hired to enliven a celebration of the Athenian invasion force embarked for Sicily. As you enter the large house below the Acropolis, you are warmed by the reassurance of tradition: the herm is garlanded with fresh myrtle; two oil lamps burn opulently at the door. In the dining room revels are already well advanced. A dozen guests recline about a table heaped with platters: archons and generals, to judge their richly woven chlamyses. A glittering hetaera shares the couch of one; two others lie with handsome boys. Slaves shuttle busily between kitchen and table, bearing heaping plates. Upstairs the women's door is firmly shut but pressed from within, no doubt, by curious ears.

A wine-quickened disputation rises above the pleasantries. The symposiarch propounds a question: "What is the highest good?" Each guest attempts an answer in his turn.

"The highest good is man!" asserts a scholarly face at the end of the table. "Not the servile scum of

Persia and the Egyptian coasts, but independent
man of Hellas, whom Thales taught to reason, and
Pythagoras to numerate the world."

"Such talk is hubris," disagrees a military type.
"Man's only claim to highness is his reverence for
the gods. They are the highest good. But you would
never guess it, to hear the blasphemies in the Agora.
Only yesterday that scoundrel, Socrates . . ."

A fleshy fellow interrupts, sputtering bright red
wine on the polished board: "I say the polis is the
highest good. Why do we launch these ships, ventur-
ing our wealth, our lives, but that our city may prevail? Do not the Spartans seek the same? The city is
the highest good because it claims, and gets, man's
highest sacrifice. Only a fool . . ."

"Please! A song!" implores the symposiarch. You
turn obediently to your flutes.

Act III: Aboard an Alexandrian round ship, one
day out of Syracuse, a clear spring morning, A.D. 60.
You are a tutor, native of Ephesus, schooled in
rhetoric at Rhodes, journeying to Rome to take ap-
pointment in the household of a wealthy senator.

Your fellow passengers are few: grubby Mediterranean merchants mostly, and Roman officials of
middling rank. One passenger you have not seen
because he keeps in the cabin aft, guarded by the
centurion's men. Ship's gossip says he is a rabbi-
tentmaker of Tarsus, the leader of a Jewish mystery
sect, charged with blasphemy and sedition, en route
to Rome for trial. Just now he appears on deck for
exercise: middle-aged, short, plainly dressed, and
balding above a dark Semitic face. You offer him a fig.
He accepts and begins to talk.

Such talk! Greek, but with a coarse provincial twang, and studded with quaint transliterations of archaic Hebrew words. Soon the two of you are in full theological debate, he thrusting blunt dialectics, you parrying with Stoic sophistry. Are there many gods or one? Is man's chief duty to his god, his caesar, his polis, or himself? Through all the prisoner's tirades runs his strange conviction that time will end, and soon; that salvation is not exclusive to a favored remnant but may be claimed by any individual of any race who chooses to believe the divinity of the resurrected man-god of the rabbi's cult; that compared with such salvation, empire, polis—everything—is dust. You make a condescending smile and have begun an intricate rebuttal when the soliders come to escort him away.

Act IV: A night in midwinter, 1644. For you, a fourteen-year-old farm boy from Zeeland with aspirations to the University of Leyden, Amsterdam is the diadem of the universe: capital of the United Provinces; dredging her canals, draining her polderlands, thrusting up her churches and municipal palaces with dogged Calvinist frenzy; her harbor crowded with towering East Indiamen flaunting the free Dutch colors; her warehouses bursting with Oriental spices, Baltic grain, Mediterranean wine, and the Low Countries' own good cloth; her streets teeming with immigrants—rich Flemish merchants on the Herengracht, exotic Portuguese Jews in the trademen's lanes, and work-hungry Ashkenazim at the docks.

You, too, sought work in Amsterdam, and found it as a printer's devil. The pay is small, but there is a clean bed in the loft and warm food on the servants' table. Best of all, the master lets you sit of nights in a corner of the paneled room above the shop, where he holds court to the intelligentsia of the town. All sorts come to puff their pipes before the great tile fireplace: merchants, painters, officers of religious wars, free-thinking Paris scholars, and sun-bronzed *schippers* from the Indies, East and West. Their animated conversation swirls about you like their strong tobacco smoke: Spanish fleets destroyed off Cuba and in the Downs; Amsterdam the capital of freedom, thought, and art, where two seasons past the Civic Guards paid Mijnheer Rembrandt van Rijn 1,600 guilders for their portrait, and only this year, on the very press below, Monsieur Descartes gave his *Principles of Philosophy* to the world. In the priest-ridden South they would have arrested Monsieur Descartes for his *Philosophy*, as they did Signor Galileo—rest his soul—for his *Dialogue*. But this is North; here Monsieur Descartes can publish, atheist or no; here reason rules, and with the light of reason—the piercing beacon of deductive thought—man, through science, will illuminate the world.

The talk flows on, as inexhaustible as the enveloping fog from the Amstel below. The Modern Age is born.

Act V: A large American city, tomorrow afternoon. You have attained the enchanted age of ten and are enjoying the most enchanting occasion of your day, the journey home from school. A familiar black limousine is parked at the tastefully barred gate of the converted brownstone. The liveried chauffeur signs the headmistress's receipt book, tosses you a friendly salute, and opens the rear door. In a roar of ignition you are off.

The park is always fun, and today it is especially exciting, still littered with placard shreds and empty tear-gas shells from yesterday's antinuclear protest. Then the fascinating university, with its fringe of head shops and denim-clad dropouts, blending a few blocks later with the evocative peep shows and massage parlors of the theatre district. You gaze admiringly at the liberated, adult world beyond the Cadillac's window. It is early, but already the prostitutes are out—pouting, high-hipped women and elegant, giggling men. Too soon the inviting alleyways of flashing neon yield to stolid, canopied apartment avenues, and the car stops. Another receipt book signature, three more salutes, a rush of elevator, one deft wave of your magnetic entry card, and the double-deadbolts of the penthouse door are sliding home again.

You select a heating program on the microwave, pick your favorite drink from the frige, then turn to the pushbutton telephone. First Alison, whom you reach through her beeper in the interns' room uptown. Yes, you ate all your lunch. No, your cold isn't worse. Kiss and goodbye. Then Joan, in her studio outside Carmel. Yes, you received the Picasso book, No, you haven't forgotten that next weekend is hers. Kiss and goodbye. You smile. Parents are much nicer on the telephone. It is better now than when all three of you lived in the penthouse, before Alison entered medical school and John-the-stockbroker moved out, had his operation, and became Joan-the-sculptress.

The day's last and best delight awaits you in the bedroom. Three dozen separate changeful universes attend your summons to creation on the giant screen: thrilling sports, spine-tingling homicide, naked love, admonishing evangelism, daring space missions, dazzling videogames—an electronic smorgasboard of diversion, as enthralling and unreal as the long ride home behind security glass. Even better, the commercials: tasty food, zestful drink, health-assuring medicines, prestigeful clothes and cars, all offered for your pleasure—your very personal, individual pleasure. As you drift to sleep you flip the channels in a sedated daze, pleased with your choice of undemanding universes, contentedly choosing that you choose.

The curtain falls.

Individualism and the Modern Age

Did I call them "acts"? In fact those five short scenes were merely fixed tableaux of the metamorphosis of Western man's perception of himself. The real action happened in between.

The giant step occurred between the Cro-Magnon cave and the brilliant, beleaguered, overripening Athens of the Peloponnesian War. It was taken by the Ionians, those primordial Hellenes who fled the Greek mainland to construct, where Europe confronts Asia, the crucible of the Western mind. Cause and effect, premise and conclusion, theorem and proof: If we would enshrine their birthplace, we must lay our laurels on the sensuous islands and abrupt, mysterious inlets of the Eastern Aegean, softly gleaming in the muted metaphysical brilliance of their perpetual Andrew Wyeth light.

The step from the cave to Ionia was irreversible. We think, for worse or better, in sequential, patterned symbols. It is the Western hallmark, our Ionian legacy. So thinking, in words and numbers manufactured and manipulated within our individual minds, we view reality as individually perceived. The cave's collectivity is forever past. The unit of perception is the self.

From Ionia our vital center recrossed the Aegean to Attica, seminating a five-decade flowering of the human mind, so much the matrix of Western civilization that most intellectual peaks and valleys of our twenty-three subsequent centuries have been mere reascendencies or desuetudes of ideas first expounded in the Athens of the Golden Age. More than their predecessors, it is true, the Athenians celebrated man as a free individual, but that freedom was only relative; they saw the individual as so indissolubly related to the group that man in isolation from his polis was hardly man at all. "[M]an," said Aristotle, "is by nature a political animal. [H]e who by nature . . . is without a state, is either a bad man or above humanity . . ." "Every man should be responsible to others, nor should any one be allowed to do just as he pleases; for where absolute freedom is allowed there is nothing to restrain the evil which is inherent in every man."

This Greek idea of freedom as a function of social constraint is dramatically illustrated by Herodotus' account of an episode of the Persian wars. Xerxes, the Persian king, has crossed the Hellespont to Europe

and pauses to review the Asian armies massed to
subjugate the tiny city-states. He summons Demaratus, a Spartan turncoat, to ask: What are these
Hellenes like? Will their small, divided contingents
dare oppose the vast Persian forces? Demaratus re-
plies that the Spartans, at least, will fight, even if they
can muster only a thousand men. Pressed by Xerxes
for the secret of the Spartans' courage, Demaratus
warns: "[T]hough they be freemen, they are not in
all respects free; Law is the master whom they own;
and this master they fear more than thy subjects fear
thee."

Although Rome substituted for the polis an
enormous state, the Romans did not revise the Greek
view of civic freedom. The Roman saw himself essentially as the member of a family and body politic,
not as an isolated individual; he understood his civic
liberty as equal access to established law, not as an
immunity against the state. But as the weight and
apparatus of Roman government came to bear more
heavily down, the thoughtful Roman felt con-
strained, if only to survive, to develop defensively a
more exalted view of his selfhood. Man's excellence,
in this Stoic teaching, resides not in his supremacy
over external forces but in his internal mastery of
himself. Happiness is maintaining correct mental
attitudes; life's only significant struggle occurs
within the individual mind.

Precisely at that turning point of history, the Apos-
tle to the Gentiles offered to the individual a consola-
tion more comforting than insulated Stoic fortitude.
Paul preached that any person could, simply by
choosing and confessing to a private attitude of faith,

transcend time and space, vanquish his own mortality, and gain everlasting life. Here was the Stoic precept of self-mastery, stretched to ultracosmic size. Correct mental attitude was no longer a mere Stoic carapace under which the oppressed self could grimly endure an enslaving world; it had become a Christian chrysalis from which the individual soul could flutter happily to a liberating heaven.

Paul's was a world-winning conviction. It so infused the West that "Christendom" became synonymous with the broad swath of earth from the Atlantic to the Urals, north from the Mediterranean as far as man was found. The new faith appeared in three successive forms: first as a mystery cult of Armageddon-expectant outcasts, huddlers in catacombs, subverters of the official gods; next as the state religion of a world empire, authoritative and magnificent; and finally as a disestablished guardian of ritual and morality within the secular nation. With each transformation Christianity seemed an apter Hellenization of Judaism, a more perfect mingling of those two richest streams of inspiration in the Western experience.

For a dozen centuries Western man occupied only the spiritual dimension of the radical individualism that was inherent in Paul's meta-Stoic view of selfhood. Theologically franchised to alter his personal destiny by a volitional act of inner belief, the individual remained content to use his newfound freedom only for heavenly purposes; the political and material implications of Paul's teachings remained latent and unexperienced within the Christianizing world. Politically, medieval man linked himself to a chain of feudal obligation as willingly as the Greek had given fealty to his polis and the Roman to his state. Materially he fixed his eyes upon treasures in heaven and did not look down for trinkets on earth. It was a paradigm of self-restraint, a paradoxical recasting of legend, in which Pandora kept shut the box, Eve abjured the fruit, and Prometheus never touched the fire.

Western man first asserted his latent worldly selfhood—opening the box, tasting the fruit, and grasping the fiery torch of Modern individualism—in the time we have labeled (with a certain unintended irony) the "Renaissance," when the stable values of the Middle Ages waned, fragmentation metastasized, and in Burckhardt's famous phrase "Italy began to swarm with individuality." "In the Middle Ages," he wrote, "both sides of human consciousness—that which was turned within as that which was turned without—lay dreaming or half awake beneath a common veil. . . . Man was conscious of himself only as a member of a race, people, party, family, or corporation—only through some general category. In Italy this veil first melted into air; an *objective* treatment and consideration of the State and of all the things of this world became possible. The *subjective* side at the same time asserted itself with corresponding emphasis; man became a spiritual *individual*, and recognized himself as such."

If the Renaissance introduced individualism as a new value into the European present, it also reintroduced two other values from the Hellenic past. One was fascination with material objectives. The other was confidence in rational thought (or, if you will, scientific method) as a means by which material objectives can be accomplished. We do not grossly oversimplify history if we view those three values— individualism, materialism, and rationalism—as the attitudinal tripod upon which the Modern Age was fixed. Certainly they are the elements from which that Age's master philosopher fashioned its fundamental myth.

It was a curious construct, fabricated by a singular man. Dissatisfied with the aridities of his humanistic Jesuit education, René Descartes found worldly insight in ten years of travel and military service, then devoted two decades of seclusion to the written articulation of his thought. His objective was material (the betterment of mankind through medicine), his technique rational—both old Greek values tried and true. It was his premise that was new. He positioned, for the first time in history, an entire thought-system on the intangible foundation of a single solitary consciousness: *Cogito, ergo sum.* His conceptual bedrock was not tablets from Sinai, or an apparition on the Damascus Road, or empirical data from external reality, but the subjective existence of the perceiver's own mind, self-sensed in doubt: *I think, therefore I am.* On this most individualistic base he erected the philosophical rationale of the Modern world.

It would be idle to speculate whether Descartes inspired, or merely anticipated, the Modern Age, but history is unimpeachable witness to the irrespressible synergism of his three dynamic elements. Harnessed by scientific method toward material objectives, in three short centuries Modern individualism literally transformed the globe: discovering continents; reordering empires; devising prodigies of technological innovation; conceiving new canons of music, literature and art; igniting two devastating world revolutions; and even—toward the Age's twilight, amid the gathering darkness of its day— pressing the frontiers of human discovery beyond the bounds of rationality and earth, to the subconscious and the moon.

With each new scientific conquest of the material world Modern man regloried in his invincible selfhood and exhorted a yet more thorough dissolution of his society into the individuals he perceived to be its constituent elements. The classic formulation of that exhortation was the essay, *On Liberty*, which John Stuart Mill published in 1859. His subject was "the nature and limits of the power which can be legitimately exercised by society over the individual." First he distinguished liberty from democracy: "If all mankind minus one were of one opinion, and only one person were of the contrary opinion, mankind would be no more justified in silencing that one person, than he, if he had the power, would be justified in silencing mankind." Regarding liberty, Mill concluded that "the only purpose for which power can be rightfully exercised upon any member of a civilized community, against his will, is to prevent harm to others. . . . Over himself, over his own body and mind, the individual is sovereign." "[T]he practical question," of course, was "where to place the limit," and it was at that point that Mill made "applications" that seem less provocative to twentieth-century readers than they did to the Victorians he addressed. His justification of individualism was more timeless: "In proportion to the development of his individuality, each person becomes more valuable to himself and is therefore capable of being more valuable to others." "[T]he only unfailing and permanent source of improvement is liberty, since by it there are as many possible independent centres of improvement as there are individuals."

A Last Hurrah

In both origin and formulation Modern individualism was a European phenomenon; although it powerfully affected other continents of established population, it struck them, like a hurricane, from without. North America was a special case. Relatively uninhabited, politically unformed, opposing no cultural breakwater to the invading tide, it was not so much transformed by the new philosophy as it was created in its image. Welcoming the most rebellious and footloose of Europe's emigrants, the United States in particular became the habitat *par excellence* of that Modern archetype, the strong, silent, solitary frontiersman, tall-in-the-saddle and quick-on-the-draw, who relished his reputation for being not merely an individual but a *rugged* individual.

The personal tastes of this new Western folk-hero were simple and consistent. He preferred his spaces far and wide. "No man should live," his maxim went, "where he can hear his neighbor's dog bark." He liked his legal rights served up in plain Tom Jefferson style, ungarnished with correlative obligations.

His economics he swigged neat from Adam Smith,
or, if the occasion called for a more modish stance, he
peered at his new, brave world through the atomiz-
ing microscope of a Milton Friedman and perceived
no connective social tissue, only separate striving
selves. For moral precept he found the laissez-faire
individualism of John Stuart Mill too namby-pamby,
and turned for inspiration to the more frankly anar-
chic self-glorification of Ralph Waldo Emerson. Mill,
after all, defended individualism on the basis of its
ultimate benefit to society; for Emerson the self-
satisfaction of the individual was justification
enough. "Society everywhere," that solipsistic poet
announced, "is in conspiracy against the manhood of
every one of its members. . . . Whoso would be a
man, must be a nonconformist. . . . No law can be
sacred to me but that of my nature. [T]he only right is
what is after my constitution; the only wrong what is
against it."

To most Americans the hyperbolic individualism
of their new nation seemed unremarkable because
their minds held no clear standard of comparison.
Their European roots were severed, and they soon
erased from the vast horizon of their isolated prairies
every trace of aboriginal tribes. In the American
Southwest, exceptionally, two antecedent civilizations survived with sufficient tenacity to preserve
contrasting estimations of the self. In Paul Horgan's
words:

> "The Indian society had always been arrested in
> an anonymous communal arrangement by the ab-
> sence of the idea of the individual. The Spanish

society was built on the inertia which allowed the high cultivation of the individual yet denied it any expression that was not in harmony with the prevailing official position of the state . . . [T]he American settlers brought a frame of life in which the individual was not only permitted but obligated to create himself socially. The forces that obliged him so were the unexampled frontier environment, the swift emergence of a self-made culture, the extension of democratic doctrine, and the joyful sanction of anyone who grew to his own individualism, comely or rude."

As the American pioneer came to personify the self-ideal of Modern man, so did the United States become the exemplar of the Modern nation. If the Industrial Revolution marched through Europe, across America it fairly raced. While thousands of farmhands were flocking to the factories of Manchester, Birmingham, Hamburg, and Cologne, millions of immigrants surged through Ellis Island to claim their futures in a promised land where all things loomed superlative—bigger, better, newer, richer, faster—and even the three cardinal values of the Renaissance grew larger than life, burgeoning into *super*-science, *mass*-materialism, and vehement, clamorous individualism. America was the very triumph and apotheosis of the Modern Age.

Also, quite likely, its last hurrah. For as the Cartesian centuries wore on something went awry. Rugged individualism proved to be more adept at forcefully winning the West than at peacefully inhabiting it, once won. Spirit-quickening technological innovation was implemented in mind-blunting assembly-line drudgery. The inspiring dream of material sufficiency awoke to the degrading reality of huckstered mass consumerism. The noble ideal of unchecked personal freedom became the base actuality of violence, drug abuse, pornography, illegitimacy, abandonment, and divorce. The very Renaissance values lost their savor. Modern man came to feel dwarfed and intimidated by his gargantuan technology, unsatisfied by the endless Niagara of material goods he so competently produced, abandoned in the lonely well of his self-isolating individualism.

A distanced future will diagnose, more accurately than our proximity permits, the mortal ailments of our times. We are too near, too intimately involved, for cool analysis. One cannot fail, however, to be impressed by the accelerating unanimity with which thoughtful observers single out individualism as the fatal miscalculation of the Modern Age. Hear these diverse voices, all speaking in that same accord:

Edith Hamilton saw our failure as the misapplication, over history, of a historic value:

"For nineteen hundred years the West has been undergoing a process of education in the particular versus the general. ... That intense individualization has molded our spirit, and it has brought to us problems new in the history of mankind, together with trouble of mind and bitter disagreement where once there was ease and unanimity. It is not men's greed, nor their ambition, nor yet their machines, it is not even the removal of their ancient landmarks, that is filling our present world with turmoil and dissension, but our new vision of the individual's claim against the majority's claim. . . .

"Along with this realization of each unit in the mass has come an overrealization of ourselves. We are burdened with overrealization. Not that we can perceive too clearly the rights and wrongs of every human being but that we feel too deeply our own, to find in the end that what has meaning only for each alone has no real meaning at all."

Christopher Lasch views our self-image as a psychological infirmity:

"[We have] a way of life that is dying—the culture of competitive individualism, which in its decadence has carried the logic of individualism to the extreme of a war of all against all, the pursuit of happiness to the dead end of a narcissistic preoccupation with the self."

Alasdair MacIntyre argues that individualism has shrunk our political options to a Hobson's choice between anarchy and tyranny:

"[T]here are only two alternative modes of social life open to us, one in which the free and arbitrary choices of individuals are sovereign and one in which the bureaucracy is sovereign, precisely so that it may limit the free and arbitrary choices of individuals. Given this deep cultural agreement, it is unsurprising that the politics of modern societies oscillate between a freedom which is nothing but a lack of regulation of individual behaviour and forms of collectivist control designed only to limit the anarchy of self-interest."

For André Malraux our glorification of the individual is synonymous with agnosticism and cultural suicide:

"The art of a living religion is not an insurance against death but man's defense against the iron hand of destiny by means of a vast communion. . . . Our culture is the first to have lost all sense of it . . . Thus, thrown back on himself, the individual realizes that he counts for pitiably little . . .

"A culture based on man regarded as an isolated unit seldom lasts long, . . ."

From many compass points, the converging accusations fly. Whether the malaise of the contemporary West is viewed from the perspective of history, of psychology, of philosophy, or of religion, the judgment is the same: The weakest leg of the Cartesian tripod was individualism, and its collapse ended the Modern Age.

I Plus My Circumstances

The most perceptive analyst of the failures of post-Renaissance individualism was the Spanish philosopher José Ortega y Gasset, the eloquent pathologist of the Modern Age. Individualism is mythology, he maintained; the individual never existed, he is an abstraction, a caricature. Apart from his community, race, or nation the individual has no real being; he is effective only as his culture gives him strength. Man is not in society; society is in man. "[T]he individual is one and the same with society; he is a node of social realities, a point of intersection, a conduit of collective energies." "[T]he radical truth is my coexistence with the world. To exist is primordially to coexist . . ." "[T]he other who lives with us is the surrounding world." "I am I plus my circumstances, and if I do not save them I do not save myself."

Listen to that enigmatic statement once again: *I am I plus my circumstances, and if I do not save them I do not save myself.* On its face that is an absurd sentence, compounded of bad arithmetic and self-consuming ethics. How can I possibly be more than myself? Surely one equals one, and I am only I. Why must I save my circumstances—whatever that means—in order to save myself? But if we examine more deeply those seemingly illogical propositions they take on an assuring significance, and we surmise within them an attitude of spirit that is an antidote to the corrosive Cartesian individualism of the Modern past and a life-sustaining credo for the post-Modern future. Let us consider carefully what Ortega's sentence does not, and does, say.

First, what it does not say. *I am I plus my circumstances, and if I do not save them I do not save myself.* This is not selling one-way tickets to Nirvana. Ortega does not believe that the cosmos is an insatiable vortex into which I must inexorably disappear. My circumstances exist, but so do I. External reality is reality, but it is not all of reality; I the perceiver must also exist to make it real. Nor would

Ortega dissolve the individual into the crowd. We cannot—even if we would—exchange our Ionian individuality for the collectivity of the Cro-Magnon cave. For Western man the unit of perception and personality is irrevocably the self. Although I am I plus my circumstances, I am nevertheless I; I am not we or it or they.

Second, what Ortega's sentence does say. *I am I plus my circumstances, and if I do not save them I do not save myself.* This is a declaration of the immutable coidentity of the individual and his world. Essentially, that declaration says that I am neither self-sufficient nor alone. I exist in time: I must pay my debts to past and future. I dwell on earth, sustained by its abundance: If I plunder my environment, I shall not survive. I am born of woman, progenitored by man; my chromosomes reiterate in other bodies: I may not excommunicate myself from either the family of home or the family of humankind. My every deed and breath compart with those of others: Absented from society I am irrelevant. My most innate aspiration is toward deity, to grasp a moral, to hear a higher voice: I am unrealized apart from God.

It is characteristic of great transforming truths that they are intuited in practice long before they are understood in theory. This is the case with the death of the individual and the Ortegan principle that man and his world must coexist. At a time when Cartesian individualism ostensibly still reigns—when the late movie each night recanonizes the lone, laconic gunslinger and graduating high school seniors solemnly declaim their Emerson as a ritual of spring—the contemporary West has in fact begun its long post-Modern pilgrimage homeward from individualism toward community. We see the community of man with nature exalted in powerful ecological movements, in the "green" parties of Europe, and in sober reappraisals of the economics of affluence. The community of men at meaningful work is championed no less fervently in influential books like *Small Is Beautiful* and in a spate of envious American analyses of Japanese management techniques. What is the revival of religious fundamentalism but man's newly rediscovered hunger for community with God?

I am I plus my circumstances, and if I do not save them I do not save myself. Like all healing thoughts this powerful Ortegan perception is both simple and familiar—as simple and familiar as the hymn we learned in the first grade. Do you remember how that second national anthem came to be composed? A college professor from New England was vacationing in the Rockies, in the georgeous American West. One morning she climbed Pike's Peak. Looking out over that stunning landscape, she had a great vision of our nation, past and future: the unmerited richness of our blessed land; our lofty ambitions and cowering frailties; the divisions and enmities we must overcome; the hurts and disappointments we must endure; our crimes and errors that must be absolved; the high, bright promise for America and all mankind we may fulfill if our youthful individualism can find mature fruition in self-responsible community with ourselves and God. Her heart overflowing with that vision of America redeemed, she wrote the verses we were taught to sing. We cannot do better, in this our

time of shattered certitudes and precarious hope,
than to remember them:

> America! America!
> God shed His grace on thee,
> And crown thy good with brotherhood
> From sea to shining sea!
>
> America! America!
> God mend thine every flaw,
> Confirm thy soul in self-control
> Thy liberty in law!

FOREIGN AID:
JUSTICE FOR WHOM?

by

W. W. Rostow

Walt Whitman Rostow

Dr. Rostow joined The University of Texas at Austin faculty in February 1969 as Professor of Economics and History. A former advisor to Presidents John F. Kennedy and Lyndon B. Johnson, Dr. Rostow has had a distinguished career in education, scholarship, and government service.

Dr. Rostow has A.B. and Ph.D. degrees from Yale University and was a Rhodes Scholar at Balliol College, Oxford University. He has taught at Columbia, Oxford, and Cambridge Universities and at the Massachusetts Institute of Technology.

In 1961 President Kennedy appointed Dr. Rostow as his deputy special assistant for national security affairs, and later as counselor of the Department of State and chairman of its Policy Planning Council. President Johnson named Dr. Rostow to the additional duty of the United States member of the Inter-American Committee of the Alliance for Progress in May 1964. In early 1966, Dr. Rostow returned to the White House as President Johnson's special assistant for national security affairs.

Dr. Rostow is the author and editor of many books. Most recently his academic interests have been aimed at producing a monumental work on the history of the world economy and a policy book with suggestions for economic change. Both books, The World Economy: History and Prospect *and* Getting from Here to There, *were published in April 1978. Dr. Rostow has also delivered a number of recent addresses analyzing the economic consequences of national energy policy.*

FOREIGN AID: JUSTICE FOR WHOM?

by

W. W. Rostow

Introduction

One of the truly remarkable features of the world since 1945 has been the voluntary transfer of resources from one government to another in the form of grants or loans on easier terms than those available in the private capital markets. This is what we call, in American political parlance, foreign aid. International organizations describe it as Official Development Assistance (ODA). By World Bank calculations for 1980, the non-Communist nations of the advanced industrial world (OECD) provided about $27 billion to non-Communist states, Organization of Petroleum Exporting Countries (OPEC) almost $7 billion, countries with Communist governments about $2.6 billion (1979). (The OECD and OPEC estimates are from *World Development Report, 1982*, World Bank, 1982, Table 16, pp. 140-141. The 1979 estimate for aid to non-Communist developing countries from Communist governments is from National Foreign Assessment Center, *Communist Aid Activities in Non-Communist Less Developed Countries, 1979 and 1954-79*, October 1980 [ER-80-1038U], p. 17.) In 1980, the United States provided

26 percent of the OECD total, a figure which fell to 23 percent in 1981. The United States produced in 1980 about 38 percent of OECD output. This proportional contribution to ODA is among the lowest.

At a later point, I shall briefly outline how this state of affairs came about. For the moment, it is sufficient to note that the foreign aid total for the non-Communist world (excluding, for example, the very large subsidies to Cuba and North Vietnam from the Soviet Union) constitutes about 0.3 percent of estimated planetary product. (Dr. Herbert Block, *The Planetary Product in 1980: A Creative Pause?*, Bureau of Public Affairs, Department of State, 1981, Appendix Table 1, p. 31, gives Planetary Product for 1980 as $11.3 trillion—$11,269,078 million—in current U.S. dollars. U.S. GNP—$2.6 trillion—was 23 percent of the global total.) The U.S. proportion of GNP was 0.2 percent in 1981. The global proportion may seem modest to some of you, as it does to me, but, clearly, $36.6 billion is not a trivial figure. Nothing like voluntary subsidized transfers of this relative order of magnitude has ever before occurred regularly, year after year, between sovereign governments in all of recorded history.

In the spirit which suffuses the Andrew R. Cecil Lectures, my purpose is not, however, statistical, economic, or even historical. It is to explore the elements of morality which, along with more mundane motives, have led to this phenomenon; to examine the present state of development and development assistance; and to try to answer, in the end, the question posed by the title of my lecture, "Foreign Aid: Justice for Whom?"

The Current Setting of the Problem

The question is of some operational as well as philosophical interest. The Reagan administration has adopted a quite lucid policy towards foreign aid. It argues, from basic premises that also suffuse its domestic policy, that foreign aid ought to be reduced. It conducted a serious review of the state of development assistance in 1981 and emerged with three conclusions which deserve respectful analysis and debate. (The Reagan administration's position on foreign aid is well summarized in the *Economic Report of the President Transmitted to the Congress February 1982*, G.P.O., 1982, pp. 185-187.)

First, the developing countries bear an inescapable responsibility for conducting rational and effective domestic policies and these should include greater reliance on their private sectors and diminished reliance on their public sectors.

Second, U.S. foreign aid programs should shift, on balance, from multilateral to bilateral forms of aid on the ground that it permits greater control by U.S. taxpayers of where aid goes and how it is used.

Third, while, in general, the World Bank and the three multilateral regional banks (in Latin America, Asia, and Africa) are given high marks for their efficiency and loyalty to serious development standards in the granting of loans, they are urged to shift their customers more rapidly from "soft" to "hard" loans and from "hard" loans to reliance on "unsubsidized participation in international capital markets"; and, in general, they are urged to pay more attention to the quality of loans as opposed to their volume of lending.

All this fits the administration's wider emphasis on private enterprise, free international trade, and free movements of private capital which, for example, dominated—but not quite exclusively—President Reagan's interventions at the Summit Conference at Cancun.

You will note that the administration did not pose certain basic questions—for example, whether foreign aid was justified at all; whether moral or other U.S. interests require an increase; or whether the whole approach to foreign aid should be substantially altered. Nor did it examine the nature of the development problems in the decade ahead and the American interest in their solution. As in domestic policy, the administration took the situation as it existed when it came to responsibility and applied to it doctrinal criteria which would tip it in a new direction, reducing somewhat the role of the public sector on an international basis, as well as at home.

The doctrinal biases of the Reagan administration have been strengthened, in their impact on the Congress, by circumstance. Policies initiated in July 1981 by the administration and the Federal Reserve (with administration support) plunged the United States into a severe recession. Amidst high unemployment, increasing bankruptcies, falling public revenues, and extraordinary federal deficits, it was not difficult to persuade men and women of the Congress, confronted by early elections, to reduce allocations for foreign aid; and that has happened.

Meanwhile, a quite different doctrine about foreign aid and North-South relations in general was being promulgated in the world—the doctrine of those who demanded a New International Economic Order (NIEO). Although it had older origins, the concept of NIEO emerged in full vigor at various United Nations gatherings in 1974. Put bluntly, it demanded of the advanced industrial countries as a matter of historical right and justice a massive increase in resource transfers to the developing regions, special measures to increase exports from the South to the North, and an accelerated transfer of technology from North to South. The initial fervor of the NIEO owed a good deal to the success of OPEC in quadrupling the price of oil and forcing a vast transfer of resources from both advanced industrial and developing countries to its members. The demonstration produced a new sense of potential power in the governments of the developing regions—thus their assertive demands on the North of the mid-1970s. But the OPEC feat proved incapable of duplication: the North successfully resisted the Southern assault, and the NIEO negotiations centered in Paris ran into the sand by 1977.

In an effort to break the impasse and produce a constructive North-South consensus, Robert McNamara, then President of the World Bank, set up late in 1977 a special commission of distinguished citizens chaired by Willy Brandt. Its report, *North-South*, published in 1980, covers a wide range of technical issues, but the heart of its argument is that large common interests require a massive increase in the flow of aid resources from North to South. The figure of an extra $20 billion per annum was cited as a target—an increase of about 75 percent for the OECD nations. This argument was rooted in an explicitly moral appeal set out by Brandt in his Introduction as follows:

"It seems to be a permanent task for man to shape order out of contradictions. Efforts to restructure international relations receive invaluable support wherever they can be based on similar values. The impulses from churches and religious communities as well as from humanism can strengthen worldwide solidarity and thus help resolve North-South problems.

"Our Report is based on what appears to be the simplest common interest: that mankind wants to survive, and one might even add has the moral obligation to survive. This not only raises the traditional questions of peace and war, but also of how to overcome world hunger, mass misery and alarming disparities between the living conditions of rich and poor.

"If reduced to a simple denominator, this Report deals with peace. War is often thought of in terms of military conflict, or even annihilation. But there is a growing awareness that an equal danger might be chaos—as a result of mass hunger, economic disaster, environmental catastrophes, and terrorism. So we should not think only of reducing the traditional threats to peace, but also of the need for change from chaos to order." (Willy Brandt, Chairman, *North-South, The Report of the Independent Commission on International Development Issues*, Pan Books, 1980, p. 13.)

This theme is buttressed by an appeal to the nations of the world—notably, the United States and the Soviet Union—to reduce military expenditures and concentrate their resources on the constructive tasks of economic and social development, including enlarged assistance to the developing countries.

The fact is that, with one exception, the many recommendations of the Brandt Commission and its moral doctrine have been ignored. The exception was the recommendation for "A Summit of World Leaders":

> "The global agreement we envisage, with the understanding that must lie behind it, will call for a joint effort of political will and a high degree of trust between the partners, with a common conviction in their mutual interest. We believe that an essential step towards achieving this would be a summit meeting with leaders from both industrialized and developing nations. Such a summit should be limited to some twenty-five world leaders who could ensure fair representation of major world groupings, to enable initiatives and concessions to be thrashed out with candour and boldness." (*Id.*, p. 281.)

The Summit, as we know, did take place at Cancun in October 1981. Its only agreement was to continue the NIEO negotiations within the framework of the United Nations. I do not know of a single knowledgeable public official, American or other, who expects any substantial positive result from them. The conventional wisdom may, of course, be wrong, and I hope that proves to be the case. But here is where we are: in a phase of contraction of foreign aid, with the central argument of the Brandt Commission essentially unheeded.

U.S. Foreign Aid: Three Motives

Before turning to a statement of my own views of where we ought to go in the field of development aid, I shall briefly review U.S. foreign aid policy since the end of World War II. I shall do so from a quite narrow perspective which conforms to the central theme of this lecture series. The question I shall ask is, simply, what role, if any, did moral values, along with others, play in the unfolding of American foreign aid policy.

I would note immediately an important distinction between personal moral values and moral values in public policy. There is in our tradition and culture what we might call a missionary strand. It decrees that individuals have a moral or religious duty to help the poor and disadvantaged. The beginning of foreign aid in the nineteenth century took the form of private support in the economically advanced Christian countries for education and medical services as well as for the promulgation of faiths in what were to become the developing regions. This missionary strand remains a serious, healing, and vital part of American life reflected in the scale of private charitable outlays at home and abroad. It would be a false hardheadedness to ignore the reality of this element in the politics of foreign aid in the United States, Canada, Western Europe, and elsewhere.

On the other hand, a conviction within the electorate that justice demands that we, the more affluent, assist those less fortunate cannot explain the origins of foreign aid in its modern form or its persistence. Two other forces have been at work.

First, there has been what might be called long-run or enlightened national interest. Will Clayton, the remarkable statesman from Houston who played an important part in shaping U.S. economic policy after World War II, put it very well in arguing for the Marshall Plan in terms of the proposition that we could not safely live as the rich man on the hill surrounded by impoverished peoples. So far as the developing regions are concerned, something like this insight has played a significant role in sustaining foreign aid over the years. The argument was not, of course, that foreign aid would quickly close the gap in real income per capita between the more advanced and developing countries. It was, essentially, that a margin of U.S. assistance would not only help the developing countries move forward in economic and social progress but also encourage them to concentrate their strongly felt nationalism on domestic development rather than on other less constructive enterprises.

This point is of sufficient importance to quote at some length a formulation set out more than twenty years ago. It comes from my *Stages of Economic Growth,* delivered as lectures in Cambridge, England, in the autumn of 1958, published in 1960:

"As a matter of historical fact a reactive nationalism—reacting against intrusion from more advanced nations—has been a most important and powerful motive force in the transition from

traditional to modern societies, at least as important as the profit motive. Men holding effective
authority or influence have been willing to up-
root traditional societies not, primarily, to make
more money but because the traditional society
failed—or threatened to fail—to protect them
from humiliation by foreigners. . . .

"[W]ithout the affront to human and national dignity caused by the intrusion of more advanced
powers, the rate of modernization of traditional
societies over the past century-and-a-half would
have been much slower than, in fact, it has been.
Out of mixed interests and motives, coalitions
were formed in these traditional or early transi-
tional societies which aimed to make a strong
modern national government and which were
prepared to deal with the enemies of this objective: that is, they were prepared to struggle
against the political and social groups rooted in
regionally based agriculture, joined in some
cases by the colonial or quasicolonial power . . . .

"Now we come to the crux of the matter.
Nationalism can be turned in any one of several
directions. It can be turned outward to right real
or believed past humiliations suffered on the
world scene or to exploit real or believed opportunities for national aggrandizement which appear for the first time as realistic possibilities,
once the new modern state is established and the
economy   develops   some   momentum;
nationalism can be held inward and focused on
the political consolidation of the victory won by

the national over the regionally based power; or nationalism can be turned to the tasks of economic, social, and political modernization which have been obstructed by the old regionally based, usually aristocratic societal structure, by the former colonial power, or by both in coalition.

"Once modern nationhood is established, different elements in the coalition press to mobilize the newly triumphant nationalist political sentiment in different directions: the soldiers, say, abroad; the professional politicans, to drive home the triumph of the centre over the region; the merchants, to economic development; the intellectuals, to social, political and legal reform.

"The cast of policy at home and abroad of newly created or newly modernized states hinges greatly, then, on the balance of power within the coalition which emerges and the balance in which the various alternative objectives of nationalism are pursued."

The case some of us crusading for enlarged foreign aid in the 1950s made was essentially that the availability of enlarged resources for development from abroad would help strengthen the hand of those within developing nations who wished to concentrate their nationalist energies on the domestic tasks of economic and social progress, thus rendering the world somewhat less volatile and violent.

In that sense, foreign aid was viewed as an instrument that would contribute to peace as well as to the improvement of the lives of the men, women, and children living in the developing regions.

But more conventional short-run criteria of national interest also played an important part in the story of foreign aid, notably, the protracted struggle against one form or another of extension of Communist power. In some cases, the linkage was immediate and direct—for example, aid in the form of defense support in which economic resources were granted to military allies in developing regions to compensate for the enlarged military budgets they bore in the common defense. In the wake of the Korean War, economic aid in this form in the arc from South Korea to Turkey dominated the U.S. foreign aid budget.

At one remove, fear of Communist penetration of Latin America in the late 1950s, sparked by the 1958 vicissitudes of then Vice President Nixon in Peru and Venezuela, as well as by the rise of Castro to power in Cuba, had a good deal to do with a shift in policy of the Eisenhower administration, yielding the Inter-American Development Bank. A still less direct reflection of the Cold War was the rallying of the Eisenhower administration to support for Indian economic development as Mao's Great Leap Forward of 1958-1959 appeared to represent a model for development which would outpace the efforts of democratic India and result in widespread emulation in the developing regions.

My point is that, in different degree and in various combinations, American foreign aid policy has been underpinned since 1945 by three reasonably distinguishable motives: the abiding missionary strand in our national character; a long-run or enlightened self-interest in a peaceful environment for our own society; and short run interests in the balance of power, notably but not exclusively the balance of power vis-à-vis the Soviet Union.

Phases of Foreign Aid: 1945-1982

Against this background, let me briefly recall how foreign aid unfolded since the Second World War. I shall do so by telling the story tersely in seven stages, with emphasis on the underlying motives at work.

(1) UNRRA and the World Bank

During World War II itself two aid institutions were created. For the short run, the United Nations Relief and Rehabilitation Agency (UNRRA) was set up to deal with urgent postwar assistance in war-devastated areas. For the long run, the International Bank for Reconstruction and Development emerged from the Bretton Woods conference of July 1944. In terms of motive, both reflected, from the American point of view, enlightened self-interest. Regions of mass suffering and delayed reconstruction might well corrode the possibility of organizing a world at peace for which Americans hoped. Thus, UNRRA had strong initial support. The World Bank was meant to be a reliable source of long-term capital, insulated from the instabilities of private capital markets whose performance had contributed to the depth of the Great Depression after 1929. Pressure from some developing countries at Bretton Woods succeeded in adding Development to its name and agenda.

(2) *The Marshall Plan*

The Marshall Plan involved a convergence of all three of the motives I have defined: a simple, direct, humanitarian impulse; a sense that American society would be endangered if Western Europe did not get back firmly on its feet; and an urgent, direct fear that unless Western Europe revived, Stalin's power, already consolidated in Eastern Europe, would be extended westward.

(3) *Point Four*

Truman's Point Four, enunciated in his Inaugural Address of January 20, 1949, had elements of missionary zeal as well as pragmatic long-term self-interest. It called for "a bold new program for making the benefits of our scientific advances and industrial progress available for the improvement and growth of underdeveloped areas . . . . It must be a worldwide effort for the achievement of peace, plenty, and freedom . . . ." On the pragmatic side, it reflected an awareness of the emergence of new nations as the process of decolonization proceeded, the pressure of the developing nations for aid as European recovery gathered momentum, and, perhaps, a sense of uneasiness about the course the developing regions would take in the wake of the already expected Communist victory in China.

(4) *The Switch to Military Aid and Support*

In the wake of Point Four, extensions of foreign aid for development purposes beyond Point Four were explored in reports by Gordon Gray and Nelson

Rockefeller; but, as noted earlier, the trauma of the Korean War shifted foreign aid policy from development to urgent strategic purposes. U.S. aid resources flowed overwhelmingly to military allies, both in the form of military aid and of military support.

(5) The Eisenhower Administration

The Eisenhower administration, aside from providing support for military allies, adopted initially a stance not unlike that of the Reagan administration; that is, it urged the developing regions to rely on trade and foreign private capital while moving as rapidly as possible toward convertible currencies. As the post-Stalin leaders in the Soviet Union began to mount quite effective, strategically targeted programs of development, responding, perhaps, to the American Point Four initiative, President Eisenhower and his Secretary of State John Foster Dulles recognized as early as 1954 that a large-scale U.S. development aid program was urgently required in the nation's strategic interest. But for almost four years Eisenhower could not bring himself to act strongly on this insight in the face of opposition both within his administration and the Congress. Meanwhile, a variety of initiatives, based on an awareness of long-run U.S. interests, germinated in the Senate, led by Democrats with some liberal Republican support. A convergence of these initiatives with a series of crises shifted the Eisenhower administration to support, in its latter years, a considerable range of new enterprises which laid the foundations for a coherent U.S. development aid policy.

The triggering crises were the Soviet launching of the first earth satellite in October 1957, with substantial psychological impact in the developing regions; the problems encountered in the Indian Second Five Year Plan; the unrest in Latin America in 1958-1959 and Communist efforts to exploit it; and the Lebanon-Jordan crisis of 1958. Out of this interweaving of long- and short-run U.S. interests came the Development Loan Fund; IDA, the soft-loan window of the World Bank; the Inter-American Development Bank; and the World Bank consortia for India and Pakistan.

(6) Kennedy and Johnson

John F. Kennedy and Lyndon B. Johnson, as Senators in the 1950s, had both played a role in the transition from a narrowly strategic to a broader development foreign aid strategy. As President, Kennedy brought about an increase of about one-third in U.S. development aid, building his rationale on long-run U.S. interests (as in the Alliance for Progress) with a strong appeal also to the nation's missionary spirit (as in the Peace Corps). In 1963, the United States contributed 62 percent of total OECD Official Development Assistance, amounting to 0.6 percent of GNP. After 1965, those figures fell off, due in part to the India-Pakistani war of 1965 (both were large U.S. aid recipients), the burdens of the war in Southeast Asia, and gathering pressures on the U.S. balance of payments. There were also some positive forces making for a decline in the proportion and level of U.S. foreign aid. Kennedy and Johnson both pressed, with some success, for an expansion of the

Western European and Japanese contributions to development assistance, including their contributions to the Asian Development Bank; and progress in some developing countries led to the beginning of some graduations from reliance on foreign aid, although not without withdrawal pains. Despite these forces, the United States in 1968 still supplied 56 percent of OECD development assistance. Development aid amounted to .04 percent of U.S. GNP.

(7) *The Seventies*

Corrected for inflation, U.S. ODA, which in 1965 had been $8.0 billion (in 1978 dollars), was $5.2 billion in 1970 and $6.0 billion in 1980. (See Table 1.) It fell between 1970 and 1980 from 45 percent to 25 percent of total OECD development aid, from .32 percent of U.S. GNP to a .27 percent. Total OECD ODA in real terms evidently rose from $15 billion (in 1978 dollars) to $22 billion. The proportion of U.S. ODA provided on a multilateral basis, through the World Bank and the regional development banks, had been as low as 4 percent in 1963. It was 16 percent in 1970 and 30 percent in 1980.

Putting aside statistics, the more fundamental facts about the 1970s are these:

The need for external resources for the oil-importing developing countries rose sharply with the quadrupling of the oil price and the recessions of 1974-1975 and 1979-1980.

To some extent, the international community responded with increases in official development assistance, including a vigorous policy of loan

Table I
Official Development Assistance
U.S. and Total OECD: Selected Years, 1960-1980

OECD	United States ODA			Total OECD ODA	
	In billions of $ U.S., 1978	Percentage U.S. GNP	Percentage Total, OECD	In billions of $ U.S., 1978	Percentage GNP
1960	5.9	.53%	58%	13.1	.51%
1965	8.0	.58	62	16.7	.49
1970	5.2	.32	45	14.9	.34
1975	4.9	.27	26	17.9	.36
1980	6.0	.27	27	22.2	.37

Source: *World Development Report, 1981* (World Bank) Table 16, pp. 164-165, except first column in which U.S. ODA is corrected by U.S. GNP deflator. OECD ODA is corrected by a collective deflator described on p. 188 of *World Development Report, 1981.*

expansion by the World Bank under Robert McNamara's leadership. In general, the multilateral lending institutions led the way in sustaining official aid flows at a time the advanced industrial countries were distracted by domestic economic difficulties.

The response of the United States was less vigorous than the OECD community as a whole, a result, perhaps, of the intense controversies and confusion about foreign policy in the 1970s.

To maintain momentum, the developing countries with access to private capital markets borrowed heavily, at high interest rates, and built up large repayment commitments which came under severe strain in the sharp recession of 1981-1982. Many smaller countries with less access to private capital markets—for example, in the Caribbean, Central America, and Africa—have suffered severely under the pressures of acute recession in the advanced industrial countries, high interest rates, and high oil prices. They experienced slow growth, stagnation, or declines in output, with actual or potential explosive social and political consequences. Meanwhile, the private capital markets, generous or overgenerous in the 1970s, are now lending with more restraint, rolling over debts where necessary to avoid declarations of bankruptcy, but much concerned by what is politely called "overexposure."

Looking back over the whole sequence, the average real growth rates of the developing countries have fallen progressively from a quite satisfactory 5.8

percent per annum in the period 1960-1973 to 2.2
percent in 1981. (See Table 2.) The latter figure implies stagnation in real income per capita. Evidently,
the policy of the Reagan administration toward the
developing regions is not of much help in these circumstances. The private capital markets which it
commends are increasingly frightened and cautious
for good reasons; reductions in U.S. foreign aid and
inhibitions on the multilateral lending institutions,
urged by U.S. representatives on their boards of di-
rectors, still further reduced the availability of
foreign exchange resources; and the sharp recession
induced by monetary policy, which the Reagan ad-

Table 2. Growth of GDP, 1960-82
(average annual percentage change)

Country group	1960-73	1973-80	1980	1981	1982
All developing countries	5.8	4.6	4.0	2.2	3.9
Low-income	4.1	4.5	5.9	3.9	3.9
China	4.7	5.3	6.8	3.0	..
India	3.5	3.8	6.5	5.6	..
Other	3.8	3.1	2.9	4.3	..
Africa	3.8	1.3	0.4	2.7	..
Asia	3.8	5.2	5.5	5.9	..
Middle-income	6.4	4.7	3.5	1.7	3.8
Oil exporters	6.4	4.4	3.0	3.3	4.6
Oil importers	6.3	4.8	3.7	1.0	3.5
East Asia and Pacific	8.2	7.5	3.5	7.2	..
Latin America and Carib-					
bean	5.9	5.4	5.6	−2.5	..
Sub-Saharan Africa	4.4	3.3	4.2	1.7	..
Middle East and North					
Africa	5.0	3.6	4.7	−0.5	..
Southern Europe	7.0	3.4	1.4	2.0	..
High-income oil exporters	8.6	8.3	4.5	−11.3	−1.0
Industrial market economies	5.1	2.5	1.4	1.2	0.2
Industrial nonmarket economies	..	..	2.7	1.8	3.0

Source: *World Development Report, 1982* (World Bank), Table 2. 1, p.8.

ministration chose as its instrument to reduce the inflation rate, has hit the developing regions in four distinct ways: It has cut their exports to the United States, reduced the prices of their exports, heightened protectionist impulses in the United States, and, as noted earlier, rendered the Congress less generous in responding to foreign aid requirements.

The developing regions, taken as a whole, are in the midst of a major economic crisis with far-reaching potential political and strategic consequences.

A Proposed U.S. Policy to Assist the Developing Regions

Against this background, the final portion of my talk will attempt to do two things. First, I shall outline briefly what I think our economic policy toward the developing regions should be. This part of my exposition will be based on the assumption that U.S. interests, moral and otherwise, require high and sustained growth in the developing regions. Second, and finally, I shall pull back and state explicitly the values and judgments which underlie my view, providing one answer, at least, to the question: Justice for Whom? But I trust that this concluding passage, by stating my presuppositions, will permit each of you to come to a conclusion of your own.

Let me begin by saying that I believe a fresh assessment of foreign aid by the Reagan administration was wholly in order. Moreover, I share its judgment—indeed, I have long argued in the same vein—that the developing countries bear an inescapable responsibility for conducting rational and effective domestic policies, and that it is time for them to ask whether they would not benefit from greater reliance on their private sectors. Government bureaucracies in a good many countries have proved relatively inefficient and self-perpetuating beyond the time when they may have been needed to do jobs the private sector could not do. A powerful "state bourgeoisie" has been created in some developing countries whose interests may not converge with those of the nation as a whole. (For a perceptive discussion of this phenomenon in Latin America, see William P. Glade, "Economic Policy-Making and the Structures of Corporatism in Latin America," No. 208 Offprint Series, Institute of Latin American Studies, The University of Texas at Austin, 1981. It should perhaps be immediately noted that advanced industrial societies have not been immune from the generation of a self-interested "state bourgeoisie.") Put another way, the balance between the public and private sectors deserves reexamination in developing countries as the capacities of the private sector have increased and government bureaucracies have conformed to the dynamics of Parkinson's Law.

On the proportion of our aid to be provided bilaterally, I am less sure the Reagan administration is on the right track. Surely, we need a national foreign aid program administered bilaterally. But the way the world is changing, with an increasing number of countries capable of participating as donors, the trend toward multilateralism begun in the 1960s should continue, and I believe, for pragmatic reasons, it will. For example, when the Reagan administration perceived a crisis situation in the Caribbean and formulated a program to deal with it, the role of certain larger Latin American countries and Canada proved politically essential and this was recognized. When we move from generalities to practical work, that is the way it is likely to be.

As for the process of "graduation" from "soft" to "hard" loans and increased reliance on international borrowing from private markets, again that process will and should proceed if—but only if—rapid growth proceeds in the developing world. But the Reagan administration's homily on this point is not very nourishing in the present circumstances of slow growth or stagnation and overloaded private capital markets.

My general reservation on the Reagan foreign aid policy is, simply, that it does not come to grips with the present and foreseeable problems of the developing world. Here, then, is my four-point program.

First, the United States must resume high and regular growth at home. Without high and regular U.S. growth, neither the advanced industrial nations nor the developing regions can prosper. Without arguing the point here, I shall simply assert that this, in turn, requires that we bring inflation under control by installing an effective incomes policy; that is, a policy in which money wage increases are geared to the average rate of productivity increase in our economy. This demands that business, labor, and government come together in a partnership of the kind that has operated with considerable success in Japan, Austria, the Federal Republic of Germany, and Switzerland. They have demonstrated that such arrangements are wholly compatible with vigorous private enterprise sectors. I am totally convinced that, soon or late, we shall have to construct in our society, out of our institutions and ways of cooperating, similar arrangements. Only then can monetary policy and fiscal policy do the jobs they are capable of doing. The exclusive use of monetary policy to try to control inflation in the year beginning July 1981 has been a barbaric venture for ourselves and the world economy.

Second, we need a coherent policy to deal with the excessive private debt burdens generated in the 1970s by a number of developing nations that will buy time for their economies to revive and that will avoid a possible general world financial crisis like the Credit Anstalt collapse of 1931. That crisis plunged the world economy into the two further years of deep depression which brought Hitler to power in Germany. To avoid this kind of liquidity crisis requires not only a large expansion in the resources of the IMF, in which the Reagan administration has recently acquiesced, to a degree, but also a structure of regular collaboration among the major central banks, the IMF, and the major private banks. The fact is that the structure of the world financial system, enormously enlarged by Eurodollars and petrodollars, is on a scale beyond the ability of the IMF and central banks to manage without the cooperation of the big private banks.

Third, there is a series of problems faced by some of the smaller countries in the world—notably, in Africa, the Caribbean, and Central America—where foreign aid subsidies are required if they are not to continue to retrogress with grave human, social, political, and quite possibly, strategic consequences. The problems of these smaller countries are not all alike. In some, the problems are starkly Malthusian—that is, acute pressure of population increase against agricultural sectors of low productivity. In others, high oil import prices and low growth in the advanced industrial countries have cut their foreign exchange availabilities and thus their capacity to sustain themselves. I believe that, for reasons of morality and self-interest, the world community must accept responsibility in such cases; and the fact is that, despite domestic vicissitudes, the advanced industrial countries and the multilateral institutions have recognized this array of problems and have done a good deal, but not enough.

Fourth, and most fundamental, we must launch a concerted long term program of North-South collaboration to deal on a functional basis with the resource problems which confront the world community now and over the next generation. This, the most distinctive part of my proposal, takes some explaining.

In mid-1972 I turned to writing a long-planned history of the world economy over the past two centuries (This effort is incorporated in the following books: *How It All Began*, McGraw-Hill, 1975; *The World Economy: History and Prospect*, University of Texas Press, 1978; *Getting from Here to There*, McGraw-Hill, 1978; *Why the Poor Get Richer and the Rich Slow Down, Essays in the Marshallian Long Period*, University of Texas Press, 1980.) At the close of 1972, the world economy experienced a convulsive rise in the relative price of grain, followed shortly by a convulsive rise in the price of energy. Set against the background of what had been happening to international grain and oil markets in the 1960s, these events and their repercussions suggested, as I worked away on my history, that the world economy had entered a protracted period of relatively high basic commodity prices for the fifth time since 1790.

Historically, the upswings were generally periods of inflationary tendency, with high interest rates, pressure on urban real wages, and a shift of income in favor of producers of basic commodities. Capital and migrants flowed to the countries and regions producing such commodities; in time, the expansion of output in the basic commodity sectors overshot equilibrium levels, yielding a protracted reversal of trends in the international economy. From this perspective, the great boom period 1951-1972 was the fourth such downswing, and we have spent the past, uncomfortable decade in the fifth trend upswing.

My perception of where the world economy has stood since the close of 1972, in the long erratic rhythm of trend periods, led to a quite particular judgment about the appropriate agenda for North-South economic cooperation. The central common task is to work in partnership to assure that the sectors supporting the continuity of industrial civilization are expanded and sustained: energy, agriculture, raw materials, and water and other environmental sectors. This requires a vast enlargement of investment in those sectors, public and private, and, so far as the developing regions are concerned, domestic and foreign. The task of this generation is to do consciously what its predecessors did, mainly (but not wholly) in response to market incentives— for example, in opening up the American West in the second trend upswing; Canada, Australia, Argentina, and the Ukraine in the third; and Middle East oil in the fourth. The task in the last quarter of the twentieth century embraces a wider range of sectors.

In the 1950s, when basic commodity prices were declining, North-South cooperation for development could focus on the need for enlarged lending on easy terms for general development purposes, with each country designing a plan responsive to its unique circumstances and its stage of growth, including its absorptive capacity. That need has not disappeared from the agenda, nor has the endless struggle to contain protectionist pressures in the industrial North. But I, at least, have no doubt that the heart of North-South economic cooperation in the 1980s—as it should have been in the 1970s—lies in the kind of functional program to enlarge investment in key resource sectors. (For an elaboration of this argument, see *The World Economy: History and Prospect*, Part VI; *Getting from Here to There*, Chapters 4, 5, 6, and 13; *Why the Poor Get Richer and the Rich Slow Down*, Chapter 7; "Latin America Beyond Take-off," *Americas*, Vol. 32, no. 2, February 19, 1979; and "Working Agenda for a Disheveled World Economy," *Challenge*, March/April 1981.)

If a sense of communal interest and communal purpose can be reestablished by enterprises in these critical sectors, I am confident that progress can be made in the other areas of mutual North-South interest. A basic requirement, however, is that the par-

ticipants and negotiators in this kind of investment
program should be officials who bear direct responsibility for policy toward these sectors in their national governments.

At Cancun, in a little noted intervention, President
Reagan showed an awareness of the need to move in
this direction. Among the five principles he set out to
guide North-South economic relations, he included
the following as his third point: "Guiding our assistance towards the development of self-sustaining
productive activities, particularly in food and
energy." Unfortunately, neither his colleagues at
Cancun nor his own administration has pursued this
insight seriously and systematically. But this is, I
believe, the large new direction in which the North
and South should move in partnership, generating
along the way large additional flows of investment in
the developing regions.

Justice for Whom?

I have spoken thus far as one who, for over thirty
years, has been involved, either as a social scientist
or public servant, in the adventure of modernization
and economic development in Latin America, Africa,
the Middle East, and Asia. No part of my professional
life has given me greater satisfaction. To play a very
small marginal role in trying to improve the lot of
men, women, and children in those striving societies
which, for historical reasons, have come late to the
process of modernization, has seemed, quite simply,
the right thing to do. I know that sentiment is shared
by many thousands of others, not only economists

but members of the Peace Corps, doctors, agricultural experts, teachers, and missionaries who have done what they could to participate in and share the difficult, often painful process of modernization in the developing regions.

But I would not have taken the positions I have on U.S. policy—and the position I have taken in this lecture—if it were simply a matter of private values.

Foreign aid, in the end, is a matter of taxpayers' hard-earned money. That money is drawn away from expenditures that individuals and families would prefer to make for their own good reasons.

Foreign aid in the past and the kind of program I have outlined must be justified in terms of the interests of the United States. In the end, it is justice for the American people that must concern us.

Why, then, do I believe that an active, forward-looking program of North-South economic cooperation is required in the interest of the American people? It is, simply, that our prosperity and security as a nation will be increasingly bound up with how the societies of Latin American, Africa, the Middle East, and Asia evolve.

We all know or sense the following rather extraordinary fact. Roughly speaking, the world's population will increase from about 4 to 6 billion human beings between now and the year 2000, and 90 percent of that increase will occur in the developing regions. What is less well understood is that their economic growth rates will be higher than those in the advanced industrial countries, as they have been systematically since 1960. (See Table 2. I explain why this has occurred in Chapter 6 of my book *Why the Poor Get Richer and the Rich Slow Down.)* The proportion of our trade with the developing regions is rising, and if we escape from the present patholog- ical state of the world economy and our own, it will continue to rise. We all react instinctively to support measures to help Mexico when our close neighbor hits troubled days. What is true of Mexico is, in fact, true for all the developing regions. The interdepen- dence of our destinies may not, in all cases, be as direct and palpable as it is with respect to Mexico, but the linkage is there and it will grow.

In short, Will Clayton's rationale of 1947 for taking the economic fate of Western Europe seriously holds now and for the future with respect to the developing regions.

But we have an even more direct concern with the fate of these regions. Put aside the Berlin blockade of 1948-1949 and the second Berlin confrontation of 1961-1962 and ask where the dangerous crises of the past thirty years have occurred? The answer is Korea, Southeast Asia, the Indian subcontinent, the Middle East, various parts of Africa, in the Caribbean, and Central America. We have fought two bloody wars in Asia and experienced two Middle East crises which brought us to hotline exchanges with the Soviet Union. Perhaps the most dangerous crisis of all oc- curred in October 1962 when Khrushchev placed Soviet missiles and nuclear warheads in Cuba. The inherent volatility of the developing regions as they pass through the process of modernization and their current and potential strategic significance account for this record of trouble. There is no reason to be- lieve that we shall be spared future crises in these regions.

I would underline that large programs of foreign aid are no panacea. They cannot wholly insulate us against the possibilities of dangerous crises in the developing regions. And, as we learned during the painful Iranian crisis of 1979-1980, all these crises will not be the result of Soviet intervention and manipulation of the explosive potentials of the developing regions. They can generate plenty of trouble on their own.

On the other hand, there is deep wisdom in the pattern of American policy which has systematically balanced the Truman Doctrine with the Marshall Plan, efforts to contain Communist adventures in Latin America with the Alliance for Progress, our struggle in Southeast Asia with efforts to accelerate economic development in Asia and to encourage the building of regional organizations in the area, and our anxieties about security in the Caribbean with a Caribbean program of economic assistance. The linkage between strategic stability and economic progress is certainly not simple and automatic, but it is real.

Returning to my three motives for foreign aid, the moral strand remains for those, like myself, who accept it as individuals; but the case for a positive program of the kind I outlined lies in a continuing convergence between our long-run economic self-interest and our abiding strategic interest in a world which provides as few opportunities as possible for exploitation—by the Soviet Union or by others—of a frustration of hopes for economic and social progress in the developing regions.

We do not now have an adequately balanced policy. In my view, neither the policy of the Reagan administration toward the developing regions nor the somewhat grandiose program outlined in the Brandt Commission report is an appropriate means for providing the necessary balance. I would hope that something like the four-point program I have outlined would do justice to the abiding interests of the American people.

Now a final word about morality. The keen listener will have noted a curious switch in the passage I quoted earlier from Willy Brandt's Introduction to the report of the Commission he chaired. He moves quickly from an evocation of the moral impulses arising from religion and humanism to a common interest in a world of order rather than chaos, at peace rather than at war.

In a world of nuclear weapons, of intense economic and political interdependence, morality and hardheaded self-interest do, indeed, tend to converge. I have long argued that the national interest of the United States consists in working with others to assure that our society can continue to evolve in continuity with the basic principles in which it is rooted. From that definition flow legitimate tasks of military deterrence and defense, but also of arms control negotiations and efforts to defuse, by negotiation, potentially dangerous crises like those endemic in the Middle East. From that definition also flow legitimate tasks of advancing U.S. economic interests on the world scene but also of using our economic resources to sustain an environment of growth in the developing regions for reasons which include but transcend human welfare in those regions and in the United States. Brandt was right in asserting that the question of order versus chaos is deeply involved in North-South economic cooperation.

It is at stake in a quite particular way in the four-point program I briefly outlined. The problems of energy, food, raw materials, and the environment that we confront in the world economy may not decree an end to industrial growth after, say, a run of 250 years from the late eighteenth century, as the authors of *The Limits to Growth* predicted. But those problems are real and still degenerative. That is, they will worsen with the passage of time unless present national and international policies change.

In the end, those policies should reflect the universal stake, shared equally between the North and South—and, I would add, East and West—in a continuity of industrial civilization which would permit us to level off in population and, later, in real income per capita when we are so minded, not by bitter Malthusian or other resource-related crises. The most primitive self-interest should, then, bring nations and peoples closer to accepting the injunction of the poet after whom I happen to be named, to which I have often returned:

> One thought ever at the fore—
> That in the Divine Ship, the World,
>   breasting Time and Space,
> All peoples of the globe together sail,
>   sail the same voyage,
> Are bound to the same destination.

THE MORALITY OF
CHECKS AND BALANCES

by

Kenneth W. Thompson

Kenneth W. Thompson

Dr. Thompson is White Burkett Miller Professor of Government and Foreign Affairs and Professor of Religious Studies at the University of Virginia, and is Director of the university's Miller Center of Public Affairs. He is Director of the Institute for the Study of World Politics and of the Ethics and Foreign Policy Project of The Council on Religion and International Affairs.

Dr. Thompson received his A.B. from Augustana College in Sioux Falls, South Dakota, and his M.A. and Ph.D. from the University of Chicago. He holds honorary degrees from six colleges and universities and was awarded the Annual Medal by the University of Chicago in 1974.

After teaching at Northwestern University and the University of Chicago, Dr. Thompson joined the staff of The Rockefeller Foundation, of which he was Vice President from 1961 to 1974. He is a Trustee of the University of Denver, Dillard University, Grinnell College, and the Patterson School of Diplomacy and International Commerce of the University of Kentucky.

Dr. Thompson has written voluminously on the subjects of politics and foreign affairs, and is the author and editor of many books. Among the most recent are Morality and Foreign Policy *(1980) and* The President and the Public Philosophy *(1981). He has also appeared in distinguished lecture series throughout the United States and in Europe.*

THE MORALITY OF CHECKS AND BALANCES

by

Kenneth W. Thompson

Most discussions of right and wrong in politics, especially in international politics, have focused on the role of ideas. Ideals have furnished the rallying point for men and nations seeking to rise above the sordid realities of conflict and power. Yet political and social theorists have differed over the relationship of ideas to politics, and in this difference two underlying philosophies have come into play.

One view has seen moral and political principles as nothing more than political ideologies, a means of making the lesser appear the greater good. Ideologies are instruments of rationalization. They are the means by which men persuade themselves and others of the virtue of political actions based on narrow self-interest. No political actor can acknowledge involvement in a naked struggle for power if the aim is mere political success. The Soviet Union describes American actions as imperialistic but justifies its own course as a necessary state in the unfolding of communism. Imperialism requires an ideology to cover its ambitions with what sociologists describe as "a tissue of lies." Some find explanations in the biological argument of preserving national existence but others turn to moral principles such as law and justice. In Gibbon's words: "For every war, a motive of safety or revenge, honor or zeal, right or convenience."

In international politics, scholars note the identification of different types of foreign policy with different ideologies. *Status quo* nations tend to call up ideologies of peace and international law. Geography and history exert their influence on the legitimacy different nations accord to different political ideologies. Switzerland and the Low Countries have historically emphasized neutrality, Britain its role as the balancer, and France the idea of security. International law must have a *status quo* to defend registered in territorial settlements following a war and a peace conference. International law in the absence of institutions of peaceful change suffers from the lack of flexibility that is possible with domestic law.

Ideologies in international relations are many and varied. Some great powers have justified themselves in terms of a sacred mission or trust. Others invoke natural law rather than positive law. After World War I, the Germans made a virtue of necessity in pointing to their disarmament and the absence of colonies prescribed by the Paris Peace Conference. Japan found the logic for its expansionist policies in the ideology of a co-prosperity sphere. Pan-Slavism was the means of justifying control over Slavs everywhere, and world revolution is defended as a necessary stage in the Marxian vision of history. The German hero was destined for ascendancy over the British shopkeeper; for Hitler there was an inevitability in the "Master Race" achieving its place in the sun. *Lebensraum* (living space) was essential for the realization of this goal. Nations may advance under the guise of antiimperialism as Germany sought to do in attacking the Soviet Union in World War II. In the

1980s, some Third World claims for a larger portion of the world's wealth and resources are couched in the language of anticolonialism despite the end, or at least the serious weakening, of the colonial era.

The United States has not been without its own more and less effective political ideologies in foreign policy. Prior to World War I, isolationism provided the banner under which America conducted foreign relations. It concealed the fact that the British navy provided the shield behind which American interests were secured. Internationalism had its birth with Woodrow Wilson in which an American President maintained that national interests were being supplanted everywhere by the common interests of mankind. In the same way that American policy had never been completely isolationist, with commercial and economic interests abroad qualifying the isolationist creed, so internationalism fell short of the Wilsonian vision. Until 1939, Hitler marched across Europe without meeting resistance because the transformational ideology of collective security was accompanied not by national resolve but by significant reductions in defense capabilities. In World War II and its aftermath, spiritual leaders such as Reinhold Niebuhr and Father John Courtney Murray called for what was called a theology of responsibility. In Max Weber's terms, their ethic might also have been called an ethics of responsibility as distinct from an ethics of conviction. They sought to stress national will and resolve above mere presidential declarations and institutions. Resting their argument on such moral philosophers as Augustine and Aquinas, they chose to place acts and consequences before rhetoric or justifications.

In international relations, the form and content of political ideologies are not independent of nations and their foreign policies. Far from transforming policies and leading to a transcendent international system, ideologies are more likely to intensify and disguise the struggle for power. Ideologies are embodied in persons (the middle class as the carrier of the ideas of liberal democracies) or nations pursuing status quo or imperialistic foreign policies. Because ideologies are justifications for state acts, there is always a gap between rhetoric and reality. Sometimes, whether deliberately or not, political actors may use ideologies as smokescreens for far-reaching political acts. However, if ideologies and rhetoric are too far removed from policy and reality, the result is a credibility gap. Conservatism and liberalism interact with one another in the play of practical affairs. More than once the United States has been saved by a liberal acting conservatively (Franklin Roosevelt and the preservation of capitalism) or a conservative acting liberally in a pluralistic world (Eisenhower in Korea and Indochina and in his warning against the military-industrial complex). Not only have liberalism and conservatism balanced one another in American political life but political leaders have used them as ideologies partly to explain and partly to obscure actions they sought to take.

The Unreality of Morality

Doubts about political ideology have led to doubts about morality and politics. For some prominent observers of the international scene, the plain facts about international morality are its unreality and deception. For them, morality in international politics measured in objective terms is a nonsubject. To invoke it is to invite cynicism or wry amusement. When questioned about the Vatican's influence on Soviet policies, Stalin asked, "How many divisions does the Pope have?" Europeans were baffled by American reactions to President Carter's moral preachments and to President Nixon's involvement in Watergate. For more temperate critics, *morality at best* is something tacked on to operational realities (a former Secretary of State described morality as "an aspect of foreign policy" without elaborating) or a strategy for making Americans feel good or a way of restoring America's position of world leadershp. It is calculation, rationalization, and self-justification concealing the taint of self-interest. Morality *at its worst* or in its starkest form, according to other critics, is crusading national self-righteousness or ideological warfare. For *1984*, it was to be Orwell's double-speak; in two world conflicts, it has been the claim of totalitarians to be democracies; most blatant of all it was Hitler's invoking national self-determination and the principles of Versailles as he swept through eastern Europe. It is old men judging young men, lordly conquerors proclaiming the sanctity of the status quo, the powerful justifying their ill-gotten gains. Religion and morality for Marxists are the opiate of the people; for the German Romanticists obstacles to enthusiasm, progress, and the survival of the fittest; for purists an excuse for withdrawal and passivity in politics. In politics, it is the cry of Boss Tweed: "What does this God business have to do with politics?"

Clusters of the plain physical facts of morality, politics and international politics viewed historically, particularly with regard to diplomacy and war, underscore the stubborn reality of *limitations* and *constraints*. Indeed the threefold legacy of history, diplomacy, and war is profoundly troubling and sobering for its evidence on the role of morality. *Historically,* in political practice, morality has been subordinated to the imperatives of politics and war. Political leaders have chosen as guides to action necessity over righteousness, dramatically portrayed in the massacre of Christians in the catacombs; the retreat from justice in Pontius Pilate's infamous phrase "I find no fault in this good man but . . ."; and the cynicism and brutality of Christian Popes and Emperors in acts of cruelty running the gamut from mere deceit to the use of court poisoners. The precepts of traditional *diplomacy* are memorable more for their candor than their uplift, as with England's seventeenth-century ambassador Sir Henry Wotton's definition of the diplomat as "an honest man sent abroad to lie for his country," Cavour's confession that "if we had done for ourselves what we did for the state what scoundrels we would have been," and Reinhold Niebuhr's conclusion that the children of darkness tend to triumph over the children of light in politics because they are clever as the fox and more shrewd than virtuous. In *war,* the Commandment "thou shalt not kill" has been crowded out by the rule "thou shalt kill for the state," eventuating in the breakdown of the laws of war. In World War II, we witnessed obliteration bombing which nullified distinctions between combatants and noncombatants. In the postwar era we have seen the testing and use of ever more lethal weapons of total destruction.

Marching to the beat of a fateful determinism, warfare's evolving technology has dictated and determined policy, not *vice versa*. Science has created its own momentum accentuated by the irresistible linkage between the development of new weaponry and its procurement and production. The grammar of warfare puts stress on two goals, victory and survival; who can ignore the threat of war hanging over every foreign policy decision? Civil war is the *exception* in national politics; warfare is the *rule* in international politics, transforming the essential context in which decisions are made. The nation-state seeks to maintain domestic tranquility and preserve the union, whereas actors in the international order aim to protect each state against loss of independence. The nation seeks to abolish conflict and maintain the workings of the political process; the international order manages conflict, manifested in the summer of 1982 in three major and eight minor wars, so called. Within nations, subnational groupings are subordinated to a more perfect union; among states, from Augustine to the present, the division of the world into independent states is seen as a moral good preferable to world domination or global uniformity.

The Morality of Political Realism

Yet the ordering of the facts of politics and international politics is not exhausted in a recitation of harsh realities and the limitations of morality. The most enduring consequence of Aristotle's definition of man as a social animal is the truth that each person gains fulfillment in relationship with others. Niebuhr began the Gifford Lectures with the timeless question, "Man is his own most vexing problem. What is he to think of himself?" If civilization in its approach to this question suffers from one grievously mistaken response, it is that produced by viewing the world through one-dimensional spectacles. We speak of man's rationality and ignore his irrationality, and vice versa. Our emphasis on virtue obscures man's sins of omission and commission: The good I would do, I fail to do, the evil I would not do, I do. Stress on good intentions conceals unforeseen consequences: The French Revolution led to Napoleonic imperialism, the Protestant Reformation to the rise of the all-powerful sovereign nation-state.

At the heart of the problem of morality is the fundamental ambiguity of good and evil destined to coexist until the end of time. Throughout western culture, popular thinkers seek to do away with the fragmentary and ambiguous character of human existence. Psychologists and liberal politicians call for ridding society of its guilt-complexes. Reformers promise the perfectability of man in which present weaknesses will give way to future perfection. The Marxist utopia envisages a new man within a new order with the withering away of the state replacing the domination of man by man and group by group. Religious fundamentalists say "believe in God and do as you please"; the followers of Adam Smith call up the image of a "hidden hand." Twentieth-century Americans, consciously or not, pledge their loyalty to a host of determinist social and political creeds.

Economic reformers, including some intellectuals of the New Deal, have lodged their faith in improved standards of living, promising not only economic gains but a happier and more peaceful human nature. Wilsonians looked to the establishment of democracy and national self-determination to assure the eradication of the balance of power and the struggle for power. Visions such as these and most political prophecies have suffered shipwreck in the turbulent waters of reality.

Yet all the constraints and negatives of human existence leave intact a residual moral dimension surrounding man in society. It is a dimension to be added to the plain physical facts of diplomacy and war. Alongside the limitations of morality, we observe another set of realities summed up in four straightforward propositions. First, man has a moral sense. Graeco-Roman thought traced its source to man's innate reason, Judeo-Christian thought to an unquenchable spark of the divine. All the world's great religions have pointed to a spiritual quality in man that persists, however diluted or fragmented. Second, this moral sense manifests itself within every human community in which men live and seek fulfillment. Its realization is most attainable in the flowering of love within the family. Beyond the family, it involves service to the more immediate and primary human communities. It can be seen in patriotism and devotion to the nation. It manifests compassion for mankind everywhere when natural catastrophes strike. Third, the task of realizing man's moral sense has grown more, not less, complex. Today's moral codes are applied not to sheep and shepherds but to vast industrial and political agglomorates. Subjects of moral concern tend to become objects not one but many steps removed. Those who administer acts of kindness and goodwill are not the Good Samaritan but big government, big management, big labor, and the super powers. Face-to-face relations are sharply diminished, yet it remains true that genuine morality assumes relations among individuals not agents. The culture has made us cynical because we know too much, doubt too much, question too much. Fourth, patient and steady acts of moral concern do not make news. We hear all too little about the thousands of man hours devoted to making society better through voluntary and civic efforts, the miles traversed in search of world peace. The hundreds of negotiating sessions which led to an Austrian Peace Treaty and the withdrawal of Soviet troops or a cease-fire and withdrawal from Lebanon are far removed from public perception and understanding.

Morality and Constitutionalism

Realism about values is also manifested within the American constitutional system. The founders saw constitutionalism as requiring a policial order based on checks and balances. They wrote of the interplay of opposite and rival interests. Constitutionalism was intended to remedy "the defect of better motives." While Alexander Hamilton defended the concept of an energetic executive and was not unsympathetic with the idea of a monarch, his views were set aside for what my colleague, James Sterling

Young, has called the idea of the leaderless state. The majority preferred a government in which authority rested in laws not persons. For at least some of the founders that government was best that governed least. Government was cast in the framework of utilitarianism; it was conceived as an instrument that would ensure those conditions under which individuals could follow their chosen lives and liberties and the pursuit of happiness.

Not only monarchy but a hierarchial structure of government was rejected. The founders displayed a mistrust of political power. As John Adams put it:

> "Power always thinks it has a great soul and vast views beyond the comprehension of the weak and that it is doing God's service when it is violating all His laws. Our passions, ambitions, love and resentment, etc., possess so much metaphysical subtlety and so much overpowering eloquence that they insinuate themselves into the understanding and the conscience and convert both to their party."

Thomas Jefferson and John Adams were respectful adversaries in intellectual contention during much of that period. Yet Jefferson balanced his unquenchable faith in the people with a clear-eyed recognition of the place of checks and balance. In 1798 he wrote:

> "Confidence in the men of our choice . . . is . . . the parent of despotism: free government is founded in jealousy and not in confidence; it is jealousy and not confidence which prescribes limited constitutions to bind those whom we are

> obligated to trust with power . . . . In questions of
> power then let no more be heard of confidence in
> man, but bind him down from mischief by the
> claims of the Constitution."

The exercise of power and the imposing of the will
of an individual or group on others was "of all known
causes the greatest promoter of corruption." However the Enlightenment may have shaped the
thought of early Americans, their views of power
reflected a sturdy recognition of both the hazards and
reality of power.

The separation of powers in the Constitution was a
particular expression of the concept of checks and
balances espoused by the founders. The division of
power among the executive, legislative, and judicial
branches of government imposed limitations on the
exercise of power. The doctrine of separation of
powers was intended to provide a check against what
James Madison in *Federalist Number 51* called "a
gradual concentration of the several powers in the
same department." It was tyranny that the founders
feared most, and the best safeguard, for Madison,
would be realized by "contriving the interior structure of the government as that its several constituent
parts may, by their mutual relations, be the means of
keeping each other in their proper places." They
went back to Montaigne and classical writers in
searching for the intellectual basis for their politics.

Students of American government have pointed to
the fact that the separation of powers was never intended as a division based on parity and equality.
This was true in particular of the judiciary. Alexan-

der Hamilton noted in *Federalist Number 78* that the judicial branch "may truly be said to have neither *Force* nor *Will,* but merely judgment . . ." He described the judiciary as "beyond comparison the weakest of the three departments of power." The executive was the Commander in Chief of the Armed Forces. It remained for later observers to note that Supreme Court Justices had only their fountain pens to hurl at offenders against the Constitution. The Congress had the power to declare war and to provide the means for raising an army. The Constitution assigned vast powers to Congress and the President over the federal judicial system, including, in the case of the Congress, discretion to "ordain and establish" inferior courts and "to constitute" them with judges whose salaries were set by the Congress but could never be diminished. Presidents, with the advice and consent of the Senate, had authority to make judicial appointments. Appropriations for the judicial system rested with the Congress as well as the power to define the jurisdiction of inferior courts and the appellate role of the Supreme Court.

Yet the Court from the time of Chief Justice John Marshall to the present has not hesitated to assert itself through its power to declare an act of Congress unconstitutional. Moreover, the separation of powers has insulated the judiciary from at least some of the political pressures which the Constitution makes inevitable. The abortive court packing plan of President Franklin D. Roosevelt testifies to the vitality and independence of the Supreme Court. Chief Justice Charles Evans Hughes responded forcefully to FDR's contention that the "nine old men" of the

Court were incapable of doing their job. In a letter to Senator Burton K. Wheeler, the Chief Justice maintained that

> "the Supreme Court was fully abreast of its work; adequate attention was being given to the large numbers of petitions for certiorari presented; . . . an increase in the number of justices for the Supreme Court would not promote the efficiency of the court [but] would impair that efficiency; . . . a plan to hear cases in divisions would be impracticable; the Constitution did not appear to authorize two or more Supreme Courts, or two or more parts of a Supreme Court, functioning in effect as separate courts." (Charles B. Swisher, *American Constitutional Development,* 2d ed., 1954, p. 945.)

The story is of course not complete, for historians have pointed out that the week following the Chief Justice's letter, he and Associate Justice Owen J. Roberts changed their votes on a crucial case prompting the pundit's comment that a "switch in time saves nine."

Constitutional provisions alone provide an imperfect picture of the workings of the separation of powers. It is more accurate to say that checks and balances become operative in a system of dynamic equilibrium. The momentum of New Deal legislation and the force of economic and social necessities brought pressure on the Court to abandon its resistance to change. It is erroneous to believe that the Constitution has decreed that the three branches of government carry out their tasks in water-tight com-

partments. Chief Justices such as Taft, Hughes, War-
ren, and Burger have played the role of "Court De-
fender" against threats to the authority of the Court.
In the same manner, Presidents and legislators have
rallied support for the authority of their respective
branches, sometimes from "a bully pulpit." The separation of powers in practice is best portrayed as a
changing parallelogram of competing forces.

In foreign relations, the flow of authority has
moved back and forth from President to Congress.
The number of executive agreements increased ex-
ponentially during World War II to remedy the de-
fects of a foreign policy hemmed in by the necessary
participation of Congress in treaty-making. (In 1939,
ten treaties were concluded against twenty-six
executive agreements. In 1941, the numbers were
fifteen and thirty-nine; in 1942, six and fifty-two; in
1943, four and seventy-one; in 1944, one and
seventy-four; and in 1945, six and fifty-four.) Edwin
Corwin's observation that the vagueness of the Constitution in locating authority for the conduct of
foreign relations was an invitation to a continuing
state of civil war between the executive and legislative branches comes closer to describing reality than
any mere recitation of the provisions of the Constitution. Not only do the comparative strengths of the
spokesmen for the several branches determine the
role they play, but historical contingencies shape the
movement of authority from one branch to another.
The powers of the presidency increase in wartime or
in time of emergency as do those of Congress following a political debacle such as that resulting from the
war in Vietnam. It would be difficult to imagine a

War Powers Act in the absence of Watergate and
Vietnam, nor is it likely that the powers of an Impe-
rial Presidency would have been as fully realized
except for the economic crisis of the 1930s and the
rise of Hitler.

Thus the separation of powers reflects not a static
condition but a situation in more or less continuous
flux. Foreign observers from de Tocqueville to the
present have searched in vain for a fixed point of
authority, especially in foreign policy at any given
time. They ask who has the controlling power. They
speak of tumult and confusion and of everything
being in motion. They remark on shifting alliances
and changing points of consensus among "opposite
and rival interests." The consequences of the separation of powers and "leaderless government" are a
continuous fluctuation of authority from one branch
of government to another, leaving outsiders who are
more at home with centralized political systems in a
state of uncertainty and confusion.

At another level of comprehension, however,
foreign observers have written about the American
system with profound understanding. They have
pointed to the American government as an outstanding modern example of a political system whose stability is dependent on an equilibrium of power
among the branches of government. No one saw this
with greater clarity than Lord Bryce, who wrote:

"The Constitution was avowedly created as an
instrument of checks and balances. Each branch
of the government was to restrain the others, and
maintain the equipoise of the whole. The legislature was to balance the executive and the

judiciary both. The two houses of the legislature were to balance one another. The national government, taking all its branches together, was balanced against the State governments. As the equilibrium was placed under the protection of a document, unchangeable save by the people themselves, no one of the branches of the national government has been able to absorb or override the others . . . each branch maintains its independence and can, within certain limits, defy the others." (Lord Bryce, *The American Commonwealth*, Vol. I, The Macmillan Company, 1891, p. 390.)

Bryce viewed politics as, in part at least, a struggle for power. His perspective diverged from the view that political life was more and more dominated by reason and that conflicts would be supplanted by an easy harmony of interests. He went on to say:

"[T]here is among political bodies and offices (i.e. the persons who from time to time fill the same office) of necessity a constant strife, a struggle for existence similar to that which Mr. Darwin has shown to exist among plants and animals; and as in the case of plants and animals so also in the political sphere this struggle stimulates each body or office to exert its utmost force for its own preservation, and to develop its aptitudes in any direction where development is possible. Each branch of the American government has striven to extend its range and its powers; each has advanced in certain directions, but in others has been restrained by the equal or stronger pressure of other branches." (*Id.*, pp. 390-391.)

The view of politics enshrined in American constitutionalism and described by Lord Bryce and the authors of the *Federalist Papers* has not gone unchallenged. Thomas Jefferson, despite his recognition of the need to control the ambitions of individuals and groups, could also declare himself unable "to conceive how any rational being could propose happiness to himself from the exercise of power over others." Isolationism in foreign policy may appear at first glance to be a noncompetitive policy based on abstention from the struggle for power. Woodrow Wilson gave eloquent expression to his conviction that selfishness and power rivalries could be banished from the relations among nations, calling for "not organized rivalries, but an organized common peace." In proclaiming government by the consent of the governed at home and around the world, Wilson declared: "These are American principles, American policies . . . . And they are also the principles and policies of forward looking men and women everywhere, of every modern nation, of every enlightened community. They are the principles of mankind and must prevail." (Woodrow Wilson, *The New Democracy: Presidential Messages, Addresses, and Other Papers, 1913-1917*, Vol. II, Ray Stannard Baker and William E. Dodd, Eds., Harper and Brothers, 1926, p. 410.)

Yet it was President Wilson, failing to take account of the separation of powers, whose vision of a brave new world and a League of Nations was defeated by the Senate, which rejected American participation in the League. After World War II, the editors of a liberal journal reaffirmed Wilson's view, saying;

"The world stands at a crossroads . . . . [One] path leads to power politics, imperialism, spheres of influence and more and more war. The other path leads to democracy, peace and freedom. It is for people of *good will* throughout the world to fight . . . for the second road." *(New Republic,* Vol. CXI, December 18, 1944, p. 821.)

Yet however appealing the philosophy of politics may be which offers an alternative to the interplay of rival and opposite interests in competition with one another, such a view did not prevail in the thinking of the founders. The author of *Federalist Number 51* maintained that "the great security against a gradual concentration of the several powers in the same department, consists in giving to those who administer each department the necessary constitutional means and personal motives to resist the encroachment of others . . . . Ambition must be made to counteract ambition." The aim of constitutional arrangements was "to guard one part of the society against the injustices of the other part." Security was to rest on a multiplicity of interests and the degree of security was dependent on the number of interests. Looking back on the work of the framers, Charles A. Beard could conclude: "The framers understood that government in action is power. They tried to pit the ambitions, interests, and forces of human beings in the three departments against one another in such a way as to prevent any one set of agents from seizing all power, from becoming dangerously powerful." (Charles A. Beard, *The Republic,* The Viking Press, 1944, pp. 190-191.)

To those who would condemn the Constitution as leading inevitably to deadlocks and stasis, the observer can point to another aspect of the Constitution. Professor Young has pointed out that constitutionalism has been balanced by what he describes as presidentialism. Periodically the nation has turned to presidential power to confront extraordinary problems. It has accorded deference to the authority of the person of the President to curb rebellions, put down domestic unrest, abolish slavery, and preserve the union. It has called on the President to lead the nation in war, to organize the welfare state, and to assure national security. Presidentialism assigns power to the leader to safeguard constitutionalism in times of emergency through the elasticity of the Constitution. The President can be as big a man as he has to be in a crisis. What is required in domestic affairs is true *a fortiori* in foreign policy, leading to Jefferson's claim that "the transaction of business with foreign nations is executive altogether." The issue in a crisis is not determined by constitutional interpretation alone but in the political struggle between the executive and legislative branches for influence and authority in each individual crisis as it arises. With the resolution or amelioration of the crisis, the powers to govern once again are judged by the constraints of the Constitution.

Human Nature and Checks and Balances

Underlying the divergent perspectives on the morality of checks and balances and determining their shape and character are two competing views of human nature. The one is based on a conception of man which stresses the duality of human nature. It affirms that man is both good and evil, rational and irrational, altruistic and selfish. Human nature has not changed fundamentally over the centuries. If men were angels, the founders had written, government would not be necessary. If men were devils, government would not be possible. Because man possesses both a spark of the divine and a trace of the demoniac, government is necessary to channel virtue and hold selfishness in check.

The opposing view of human nature awaits with confidence the emergence of the new man. For Marxists, the new man will be born with the creation of a genuine socialist order. For heirs of the Enlightenment, reason will triumph with the spread of democracy and education. The rivalries and conflict of earlier periods in political history are seen as no more than a passing stage in man's evolution. The struggle for power of rival and opposite interests in politics, to the extent it persists, represents a cultural lag in mankind's irresistible march from a primitive to a modern scientific age. At present, man pursues a double standard of conduct in his private and his public life. Privately, man is honest and ethical; publicly he covers his acts with a tissue of lies and deception. His virtue in personal relations is seen as an outgrowth of the conquest of culture over barbarism and of a moral over an immoral age. At an earlier stage in man's evolution, his conduct in private affairs was corrupted by strife and violence. Through reason, man has progressed from conflict to cooperation in personal relations and in organized domestic politics. The one remaining cultural lag is being eradicated in the area of international politics. The same conception of ethics which determines the conduct of individuals is in process of shaping the way nations behave in one universal world community. The forward march of history is carrying nations from a retarded condition into a new and enlightened era when private standards will become public rules.

Seen from the perspective of the realist view of human nature, belief in the transformation of human nature is misplaced. Man's ambition for influence and power and hence the enduring character of competition with his fellowman is inherent in the human condition. It is utopian to assume that either men or nations will soon abandon old forms of politics and world politics without having something else to put in its place. There is a wide gulf between political actions and the ideological rationalizations in which they are cloaked. National leaders declare that their aim is to offer freedom or communism to the rest of the world. Power is essential to this end. In the process, one nation's power inspires fear and anxiety in other nations seeking their own self-preservation and survival. Because of a Hobbesian fear, nations in their quest for security achieve power and influence at the price of security in other groups. Tragically, there is no alternative to the morally hazardous quest for security through power. This principle is expressed in each generation by moral, logical, and sentimental arguments which acquire the authority of doctrine.

Within and among states, it is fashionable to deny the central place of political rivalries and power conflicts. Some of the culture's wise men have dreamed of a purely rational adjustment of interests in society or have looked to the assuagement of rivalries and differences through scientific solutions or by sharp definitions and distinctions of justice and injustice. Thus a hiatus grows up between the shrewd concepts of practical men of affairs and the vapid speculations of utopian philosophers. By contrast, the early founding American statesmen were imbued with political and historical insight concerning political power and the balancing of power.

From the standpoint of the realists' conception of human nature and politics, the separate units in all societies composed of autonomous members owe their existence primarily to the success of the balance of power and a system of checks and balances. Unless one component unit is prevented from gaining ascendancy over the others, the political system will ultimately be shattered or destroyed. It is common to human existence and to animal life in general that when any member or group seeks to increase its influence and power beyond the point where equilibrium with its rivals can be preserved, either the rivals will give way and disappear or else, by combining, will keep the expansionist force in its place. With animal life the process is often unconscious and automatic, but in politics and diplomacy effectiveness depends on those sharp discriminations and informed calculations by which the statesman perceives crucial changes in the equilibrium of power. A steady view of human nature, the recurrent patterns of political rivalries, and the necessity to keep political competition in check all point to the perennial need for balances of power and checks and balances in politics.

The Ethics of Checks and Balances

Because of the nature of man and of politics, statesmen and nations never wholly escape the judgment of elementary ethical standards. The history of politics makes plain that no people have ever completely divorced politics from ethics. Man for the most part seeks to conform to standards more inclusive than mere success. As we have seen in considering ideologies, political actors justify themselves in moral terms in most societies and cultures. They pay tribute to some kind of moral order with consequences both in words and deeds. In politics, a striking dialectical movement occurs between expediency and morality. Practical political moves are articulated with an eye to moral principles. In however limited and fragmentary a way, acts of political expediency are seen to carry forward aims of justice and the common good. Thus political morality forces the statesman who would link expediency with ethics to choose political measures so that the practical and moral march hand in hand.

Certain basic assumptions undergird checks and balances in American constitutionalism and balance or equilibrium in world politics. One assumption is that the maintenance of a pluralistic society is preferable, for the present at least, to its destruction. Another assumption is that some type of orderly change through the workings of a particular political process is more desirable than radical and disruptive change. To the extent that the individual is considered to be of primary importance in politics, individual rights are more likely safeguarded. Harking back to the Greeks, balance and moderation, rather than domination and extremism, are defined as political virtues. Not only the individual but minorities will be protected by checks and balances. The author (Hamilton or Madison, according to different historians) of *Federalist Number 51* recommended

> "comprehending in the society so many separate descriptions of citizens as will render an unjust combination of a majority of the whole very improbable, if not impracticable . . . The society itself will be broken into so many parts, interests, and classes of citizens, that the rights of individuals, or of the minority, will be in little danger from interested combinations of the majority."

John Stuart Mill set forth the ethical basis of such a system in more explicit terms saying:

> "In a state of society thus composed, if the representative system could be made ideally perfect, and if it were possible to maintain it in that state, its organization must be such that these two classes, manual laborers and their affinities on one side, employers of labor and their affinities on the other, should be, in the arrangement of the representative system, equally balanced, each influencing about an equal number of votes in Parliament; since, assuming that the majority of each

class, in any difference between them, would be mainly governed by their class interests, there would be a minority of each in whom the consideration would be subordinate to reason, justice, and the good of the whole; and this minority of either, joining with the whole of the other, would turn the scale against any demands of their own majority which were not such as ought to prevail." (John Stuart Mill, *Consideration on Representative Government*, Henry Holt and Company, 1822, p. 142.)

If Mill's optimism regarding minorities reflects the spirit of his age, his statement is nonetheless a further elaboration of the ethics of divided power. In the world of politics, the best man can hope for is some type of distributive justice. Robert Frost wrote that "good fences make good neighbors." In all the more contentious arenas of life, the principle of the fence dividing those struggling to advance their own interests remains a symbol of proximate justice. In every human community, lines of demarcation are drawn to designate the areas of authority and jurisdiction each party claims. If such justice falls short of the higher and nobler formulations of abstract justice, it has at least the virtue of endeavoring "to give each man his due."

The system of checks and balances in the American Constitution and the international balance of power rest on common intellectual and political foundations. The same motive forces in politics gave rise to both. Both undertake to provide some measure of order and stability and to safeguard the independence of their component parts. Both go back to the same theory of human nature. Both are subject to the same dynamic process of change. In both, the political actors achieve equilibrium, are threatened by disequilibrium, and search for new balances of power in response to new social forces. Both are deserving of study and reflection, then, not as outmoded forms of political order but as perennial realities of politics.